Flowering Shrubs and Small Trees for the South

Marie Harrison

Pineapple Press, Inc.
Sarasota, Florida

Inquiries should be addressed to:

Pineapple Press, Inc.
P.O. Box 3889
Sarasota, Florida 34230

www.pineapplepress.com

Library of Congress Cataloging-in-Publication Data

Harrison, Marie, 1942-
Flowering shrubs and small trees for the South / Marie Harrison. --
1st ed.
       p. cm.
Includes bibliographical references and index.
ISBN 978-1-56164-439-1 (pbk. : alk. paper)
1. Flowering shrubs--Southern States. 2. Flowering trees--Southern
States. I. Title.
SB435.52.S67H36 2009
635.9'760975--dc22
                                        2008033821

First Edition
10 9 8 7 6 5 4 3 2 1

Design by Shé Hicks
Printed in the United States of America

Contents

Chapter 3
Herbaceous or Semiwoody Shrubs   110

Chapter 4
Other Trees and Shrubs

Trees

Shrubs

Acknowledgments

Few book-length works on the subject of plants are solitary pursuits. This one is no exception, for many people have made major contributions. Images of plants in this book have come from all over the country. Many I took myself, but many others were contributed by people whom I have never met.

Special recognition goes to the University of Georgia and the Warnell School of Forestry and Natural Resources. Their website at www.bugwood.org has been the source of many of my pictures. Thanks to all of the people who contributed to this website and granted permission for me to download their images.

Other help has come from Wayside Gardens, Park Seed Company, and Proven Winners, who have allowed use of their beautiful images. Much gratitude goes to the USDA-NRCS Plants Database and to Wikipedia Commons, as well as to many individuals who willingly shared their pictures. The artistic talents of illustrator Joe Stoy add the finishing touches.

Before this manuscript went to the publisher, it was edited by three talented friends—Vivian Justice, my English teacher friend, found some dangling participles and a bit of disagreement among the subjects and verbs; Val Boyles and Kathy Gresko, fellow master gardeners, read through the manuscript and offered valuable insights and suggestions.

Members of the gardening public who have purchased and read my previous books and who are looking forward to this one are a necessary part of the equation. Pineapple Press has polished, designed, and edited again to make the finished product the best it can be. Then, of course, there's Amiable Spouse, my best and closest friend. Without his patience, tolerance, and support, none of this would have happened.

The collaborative efforts of everyone have made this book possible. It all adds up to a book that I hope will be useful to many people who are considering adding flowering trees or shrubs to their landscapes.

Aesculus pavia (Red Buckeye)

Introduction

Is it a Tree or a Shrub?

Trees and shrubs make up the backbone of the garden. Flowering trees and shrubs add an element that is difficult to attain with any other kind of plant. Often their bloom cycle is short, sometimes lasting for only a week or two. Too many that bloom at the same time might make the landscape confusing or too busy, but well-placed blooming shrubs or trees selected to bloom at different times of the year can make the difference between a humdrum landscape and one that is spectacular.

Often it is difficult to decide the differences between trees and shrubs. Initially, one thinks that a tree is large and a shrub is small. The line begins to blur, however, when comparing the differences between large shrubs and small trees. Actually, the pruning and training methods employed are often the determining factors.

When selecting flowering shrubs and trees for the landscape, remember that you will need to choose the proper size plant, to meet its cultural needs, and to provide for its upkeep. The cardinal rule is "right plant, right place." If chosen wisely, planted correctly, and pruned using proper techniques, your trees and shrubs should contribute lasting beauty to your landscape.

Planting Basics

Correct planting methods are vital to the welfare of plants. The University of Florida suggests very specific procedures for planting container-grown trees. Dig the planting hole about one and one-half times the diameter of the root ball (wider if the soil is wet or compacted) and not quite as deep as the container is tall. Next, find the point where the topmost main root emerges from the plant's trunk. You may actually have to dig into the potting medium to find this root since it may have been planted too deeply in the nursery container. Find a main root comparable in diameter to some of the plant's limbs. After this topmost root is located, place the plant in the hole so that the main root is at the soil surface after the plant has been planted. It is better to plant too shallowly than too deeply. As you fill in around the ball, slice the shovel down into the loose soil several times and water thoroughly to remove air pockets.

Do not mound soil over the roots, but form a saucerlike catchment basin around the edge of the root ball with mulch to facilitate watering. Mulch with a three- to four-inch layer of organic material to buffer soil temperature, reduce weed competition, and conserve moisture. Do not cover the root ball with mulch, but apply it all around the root ball and out far enough so that the area under the dripline is mulched. Retain the mulch out to the dripline, and remember that this area will increase as the tree grows.

Adding organic matter to the soil is not recommended. Researchers at the University of Florida have found that this practice may actually hamper tree growth by keeping the roots from spreading out into the native soil. However, watering is extremely important. Newly planted trees should be kept moist until the plants are well established. During the first week, trees should be watered daily. Then for the next four to six weeks, they should be watered every other day. From seven to twelve weeks after planting, trees should be watered once a week. Watering until the root ball and surrounding soils are thoroughly wet at each irrigation is recommended. This will encourage deep root systems. Fertilization should begin a few months after planting. A light application of slow-release fertilizer will encourage healthy growth.

Similar guidelines should be followed when planting shrubs. The major difference concerns the size of the plants. Amending the soil for a shrub would be much easier because the amount of soil that must be altered is much less. Nevertheless, if the soil is amended, the amendments should be incorporated over the entire area where the shrub's roots will eventually grow. Very little benefit will be realized if a small hole is dug and amendments added to it.

Dealing with Pests and Diseases

Keeping trees and shrubs healthy and meeting their needs for sunlight, nutrients, and water are the best defenses against insects and diseases. Dr. Ed Barnard, forest pathologist at the University of Florida, says that insects generally attack trees that are under some kind of severe environmental stress, have sustained some major injury, or are already dead. By the time such damage is noticed, it is too late to save the tree. Extension offices throughout the South can advise about insect and disease control.

Pruning Basics

A newly planted tree should not be pruned; it needs every leaf it has to produce food for good root growth. Exceptions are dead or broken limbs, injured branches, or branches that cross and rub each other. Prune these back to a healthy stem or branch and leave no stubs. Never, ever top a tree or cut back its top-most growing point. Doing so will destroy the tree's natural form and make it more prone to weak growth and pests.

A few things should be pruned routinely. Remove suckers (fast-growing stems that grow from the roots or from the base of the trunk) as they occur. Limbs that sag or grow too close to the ground can be removed as needed for clearance. Branches that form acute angles (45 degrees or less) from the trunk form weak attachments and will break easily in high winds or under the weight of snow and ice. Watersprouts (vigorous shoots that grow straight up from the trunk or branches) should be cut out. Likewise, limbs that die, become diseased, or are broken should be removed as soon as possible. Prevent damage by removing a branch that crosses another one and rubs against it. Remove limbs that compete with the central leader of the tree so that only one main leader is present. Remove any branches that are too close or that are not well-spaced in a generally spiral arrangement around the trunk.

Proper removal of large branches requires three separate cuts. The first cut is made on the lower side of the branch about 15 inches away from the trunk and as far up through the branch as possible before the branch weight begins to bind the saw. The second cut is made downward from the top of the branch about 18 inches from the main trunk, which causes the limb to split cleanly between the two cuts without tearing the bark. The remaining stub is easily supported while it is cut from the tree.

Removal of the stub is often the killing blow. Before making this last pruning cut, one should find the branch bark ridge. It is usually rough and always darker than the surrounding bark and is obvious on most species. Next, locate the branch collar, which is the swelling beneath a branch. The final cut should begin just outside the branch bark ridge at the top of the branch. From there it should angle to just outside the branch collar at the bottom of the branch. Never make a flush cut.

Research has proven that painting wound dressing on the cut is not a beneficial practice. Often, when exposed to the sun and weather, the protective coating cracks, allowing moisture to enter and accumulate in pockets between the wood and the wound covering. This situation may be more inviting to wood decay organisms than one with no wound dressing.

Explanation of Data

For the reader's convenience, I have included certain data for each plant. Data include:

Scientific name: The genus and species (binomial). This name is the same throughout the world. A person should be able to take this name and identify the plant to a nurseryman or other person without the worry of mistaken identity. Plants are arranged in each section in alphabetical order according to the scientific name. (See Family on p. 13.)

Common names: The second listing on each page is the most frequently used common name. Other common names by which a plant may be known are listed under "Other name/s." These names vary, and the reader may know even more common names by which many of the trees and shrubs included are known.

Pronunciation: An acceptable pronunciation is given, based on sources from the University of Florida, Botanary (an online botanical dictionary), and those found in other reliable books and magazines. There are no hard and fast rules governing the pronunciation of botanical names. In his book *Botanical Latin,* William Stearn stated: "Botanical Latin is essentially a written language, but the scientific names of plants often occur in speech. How they are pronounced really matters little provided they sound pleasant and are understandable by all concerned."

Hardiness: Plant hardiness rating is based on those defined by the United States Department of Agriculture Plant Hardiness Zone Map (USDA Miscellaneous Publication No. 1475, issued January 1990 as authored by Henry M. Cathey while director of the U. S. National Arboretum).

Salt tolerance: Salt tolerance ratings for plants are listed as unknown, none, slight, moderate, and high. Definitions are in line with those described by the University of Florida as follows:

None: Plants are not known to be salt tolerant. No data was available to indicate tolerance to salt.

Slight: Slightly salt tolerant plants have poor salt
tolerance and should be always used well back
of exposed areas and be protected by buildings,
fences, or plantings of more salt-tolerant species.

Moderate: Moderately salt-tolerant plants tolerate
some salt spray but grow best when protected
by buildings, fences, or plantings of more salt-
tolerant species.

High: Highly salt-tolerant plants are resistant to salt
drift and can be used in exposed locations.

Unknown: No data was found to substantiate
tolerance or intolerance to salt.

Salt tolerance relates to a plant's resistance to and ability to
grow under conditions of high winds, salt spray, alkaline soils,
and infertile, sandy soils. If any of these four conditions becomes
extreme, the tolerance of a given plant to salt may be affected.

Family: Scientific and common name of family to which plant
belongs. Scientific names used in this book are based on the APG
II (Angiosperm Phylogeny Group) system of plant classification.
This modern system of plant taxonomy was published in 2003
and represents the broad consensus of a number of systematic
botanists. Their work reflects new knowledge found by examining
the molecular structure of plants. Of great assistance was the
GRIN (Germplasm Resources Information Network) website,
which allows an easy search for the family and generic names of
hundreds of plants named according to the APG II system.

Size of plant: The height and width of each plant is given,
but it is based on averages. Actual size may vary according to
planting site, area of the country, soil, fertilization, and other
factors. Most trees are variable in form. When planted in groups or
in small openings, they assume a form more upright than average.
Conversely, trees planted in open areas with plenty of room to
grow will develop a broader crown and will not grow as tall as
specimens the same age that are planted in crowded conditions.

Origin: The country or place of origin is given, or the part of
the world to which the plant is native.

Propagation: The most frequently used means of propagating
each plant is listed.

Note: Photographs are of the species (or hybrid or cultivar) of
the main entry name unless otherwise captioned.

What's in a Name?

Written by Leona Venettozzi (1924–2005)*

Leona Venettozzi was a highly respected horticulturist and Flower Show School instructor of horticulture for National Garden Clubs.

The binomial system of plant classification was a great breakthrough when Linnaeus proposed it and it was put into use. And there it has remained—the genus and the species, and no other plant ever has the same name. Considering the chaotic condition of nomenclature prior to Linnaeus, it was indeed a monumental advance. Carolus Linnaeus (1707–1778) was a great Swedish botanist, often called the father of nomenclature and classification of living organisms.

Common names are often useless for scientific purposes. The common name of a plant would be called by its name in the language of the person using it, and that same plant would be called by another name in another language. Further, the same plant, in the same language, might be called by different common names in other parts of the same state or country. For scientific purposes you can imagine the problems this created. But, with one plant having a genus and species name that no other plant has, regardless of where in the world the plant might live, be grown, or get talked about, it would not be confused with any other.

This is the **binomial system**, whereby a plant is called by two names: the first, the genus and the second, the species. (The genus is always capitalized while the species is written with a lowercase first letter.) Following the genus and species, there will be an initial or abbreviation which indicates the scientist who first described and named the species. (Ex.: *Rosa setigera* Mich., by Andre Michaux, or *Zea mays* L., named by Linnaeus.)

The advantage of scientific names is that they are governed in part by rules of international congresses of biologists and therefore are uniformly regulated and are based on Latin and Greek words, making an international scientific language, recognizable worldwide.

Biologists give scientific names based on different things. A genus or species name may be called after the Greek or Latin name for that particular group of plants, e.g., *Quercus* for the oaks and *Pinus* for the pines. Sometimes, the name honors a public figure or famous scientist, e.g., the genus *Washingtonia* (Palms), or the name might honor a person, as with the species name *blossfeldiana* or *michauxiana.* Often genus and species names describe some conspicuous feature of a plant—*Liriodendron tulipifera* indicates a tree (*-dendron)* that bears (*-fera)* tulip-like flowers (*-tulipi).*

Other common species names indicate color of the foliage or flowers—*rubrum* (red), *alba* (white), *purpurea* (purple), etc. The species name may describe some habit or characteristic, such as *prostrata* (prostrate, or lying on the ground), *lanceolata* (lance-shaped), *globosa* (round or globe-shaped), etc. Species names may indicate the area (*canadensis, virginiana, siberica*) of origin or habitat (*aquatica, maritima, saxicola*).

(*Used with permission of her children, Tina V. Tuttle, Gina V. Jogan, David J. Venettozzi, and T. Mark Venettozzi)

A Bit More Information on Plant Names (by the author)

A cultivar (cultivated variety) is a plant that is selected because it is significantly different from the rest of the species. This difference may be deliberately caused by man's manipulation or it may occur naturally. Usually the cultivar name is an English word, so it is not italicized, but the first letter of each word is capitalized and the word is enclosed in single quotation marks. An example is *Buddleja davidii* 'White Bouquet'. Sometimes distributors of plants ignore the cultivar name and assign their own name for a plant to make it more marketable. For example, *Kolkwitzia amabilis* 'Maradco' was renamed Dream Catcher. This trademark name is followed by ™or ®. Correct notation is *Kolkwitzia amabilis* Dream Catcher™ 'Maradco'.

Further subcategories used by botanists include subspecies (subsp.), variety (var.), and forma (f.). Usually one or the other is used, and the abbreviation of the category is used as well. Examples are *Magnolia sieboldii* subsp. *japonica, Loropetalum chinense* var. *rubrum,* and *Salix babylonica* f. *rokkaku.*

Sometimes two species are crossed, sexually producing offspring. The scientific name is then written as a formula. *Abelia* ×*grandiflora* is a cross between *A. chinensis* and *A. uniflora.*

15

Furthermore, two different genera may be crossed. In this case a multiplication sign "×" is placed before the name of the plant. Leyland Cypress is ×*Cupressocyparis leylandii*. It is the child of *Cupressus macrocarpa* and *Chamaecyparis nookatensis*.

It is easy to understand why scientific names are important. Common names are fine for everyday conversation, but if we ask the nursery to order a plant for us, a scientific name is necessary. If we simply ask for a buckeye, we might get a Texas buckeye, a California buckeye, a yellow buckeye, or any of several others in the *Aesculus* genus. To be sure that we get the plant we want, we must use the scientific name.

Some plants listed in this book should be avoided or used with caution because of their potential invasiveness. Plants marked with "*Caution" have proved to be invasive in some parts of the country. However, just because a plant is invasive in one part of the country does not necessarily mean that it is invasive everywhere. Be aware of these cautions, and check with an extension office or consult your state's list of exotic invasive pest plants if you are in doubt. Other valuable information is available from the following organizations:

Southeast Exotic Pest Plant Council (SEEPPC)
Mid-Atlantic Exotic Pest Plant Council (MAEPPC)
USDA Forestry Service
Plant Conservation Alliance
National Wildlife Federation
National Association of EPPCs
The Nature Conservancy
IFAS Assessment of Non-Native Plants in Florida's Natural Areas

USDA Hardiness Zone Map

Hardiness ratings in this book are based on those established by the United States Department of Agriculture. It is USDA Miscellaneous Publication No. 1475, which was issued January 1990.

This book is intended primarily for gardeners in USDA Zones 7, 8, and 9 of the southern United States. However, gardeners in other zones may find some information pertinent to their areas.

Keep in mind that the map is only a guide. Additional factors, such as soil type and fertility, soil moisture and drainage, exposure to sun and wind, humidity, and many others influence a plant's success or failure in the garden. Often microclimates in an area allow plants to be grown beyond the hardiness range suggested by the map. Global warming may also be a factor that allows plants to be grown beyond the areas indicated.

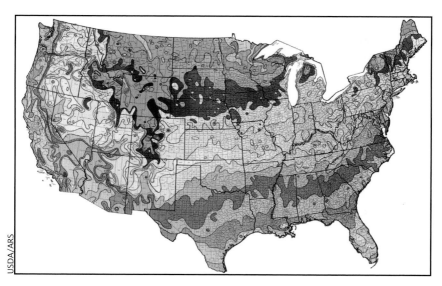

USDA/ARS

Zone Temperature

Zone	Temperature
1	Below –50 F
2a	–45 to –50 F
2b	–40 to –45 F
3a	–35 to –40 F
3b	–30 to –35 F
4a	–25 to –30 F
4b	–20 to –25 F
5a	–15 to –20 F
5b	–10 to –15 F
6a	–5 to –10 F
6b	0 to –5 F
7a	5 to 0 F
7b	10 to 5 F
8a	15 to 10 F
8b	20 to 15 F
9a	25 to 20 F
9b	30 to 25 F
10a	35 to 30 F
10b	40 to 35 F
11	above 40 F

The most recent plant hardiness map from the United States Department of Agriculture was published in 1990. Work is progressing on a new version that will be web based, digital, and interactive. Check the USDA website (http://www.usna.usda.gov/Hardzone/ushzmap.html) for the new map due out soon.

Chapter 1

Small Flowering Trees

Exactly what constitutes a "small" flowering tree is often a matter of opinion. In many instances, how a plant is pruned and trained determines whether it is a shrub or a tree.

In this section, most of the trees selected grow within the 15- to 30-feet-tall range, though there are some exceptions. All bear flowers, but some have other attractive features as well. Some have colorful foliage, attractive fruits, handsome bark, or other attributes that add to their appeal. While a few of the trees are evergreen, most are deciduous. Some should be avoided or used with caution. Dooryard fruit trees are not included. Although some of the plants bear edible fruits, they have been included mainly for other ornamental qualities.

Red buckeye welcomes ruby-throated hummingbirds to the garden.

John D. Byrd

Strawberry tree is evergreen and has flowers, showy fruits, and handsome bark.

Aesculus pavia

Red Buckeye

Say: ES-kew-lus PAH-vee-uh (or
  PAY-vee-uh)
Salt tolerance: Slight
Size: 15–20 ft. tall/15–20 ft. wide
Origin: Southeastern United States
Hardiness: USDA Zones 5–9

Family: Sapindaceae (Soapberry)
Other names: Firecracker plant,
  scarlet buckeye
Propagation: Fresh seeds; woody
  stem cuttings

red buckeye usually remains a shrub or small tree not more than ten feet tall. However, in the northern extent of its range it may reach 25 feet tall.

Red buckeye can be used as a novelty patio tree or as part of a shrubbery border. Branches develop near the ground, but they can be removed for a more treelike appearance, if desired. Trees lose leaves as early as August but leaf out very early in the spring.

A few cultivars of red buckeye can be found. 'Atrosanquinea' has deeper red flowers, and 'Humilis' is a low or more prostrate shrub with red flowers in small clusters. Variation in the species is tremendous, and some plants have yellow or white flowers.

Early in February the red buckeye starts leafing out. Opposite, compound leaves with five to seven leaflets make identification easy. Leaves have dark red petioles (leaf stalks) and central veins.

Three- to six-inch elongated clusters (panicles) of bright red flowers bloom at the tips of the branches in early spring and attract early-returning ruby-throated hummingbirds. Round, one- to two-inch brown seeds attract squirrels and mammals but are toxic to humans and pets. Planted in moist soil, seeds will germinate easily and plants will begin flowering after about three years. In the Deep South

Culture Red buckeye is at home in rich deciduous woodlands, low mixed hammocks, and river banks throughout the South. It prefers moist, well-drained soil and partial sun, and is at its best as an understory plant. When planted in the landscape, water often until it is established and as needed thereafter to maintain soil moisture. Protect from hot afternoon sun, and avoid planting in a place where salt-laden breezes will cause the leaves to burn. Mulch well with organic mulch. Fertilize lightly when growth starts in early spring. No pests or diseases are of major concern.

Caution*
Albizia julibrissin
Mimosa

Say: al-BIZ-ee-uh joo-lih-BRISS-in
Salt tolerance: Slight
Size: 15–25 ft. tall/25–35 ft. wide
Origin: Asia
Hardiness: USDA Zones 6B–9

Family: Fabaceae (Bean)
Other names: Silk tree, powder puff tree
Propagation: Seeds (contribute to its invasiveness)

Culture Mimosa grows best in full sun and in almost any soil. It is drought tolerant but has a better appearance with adequate moisture. The tree is beset with a number of problems. Blooms, leaves, and seedpods create a considerable litter problem. Wood is brittle and does not hold up well in high winds. Mimosa wilt is prevalent in parts of the country and has killed many trees. Insects that attack this tree include cottony cushion scale, mites, and mimosa webworm.

A healthy mimosa tree in bloom is a spectacular sight. The low branching, open, spreading habit and lacy, fernlike foliage are attractive in themselves, but the real beauty comes when the silky pink pompom blossoms bloom.

Despite the beauty of the mimosa, it should be avoided. Over much of the South this tree seeds freely and invades any type of  disturbed habitat, including old fields, stream banks, and roadsides. Once established, trees are difficult to control because the long-lived seeds germinate readily and cut trees resprout vigorously. As a strong competitor for sunlight and nutrients, it inhibits the growth of more desirable native species.

Lists to Consult
Florida Exotic Pest Plant Council (FLEPPC), Southeast Exotic Pest Plant Council (SEEPPC), USDA Forestry Service, National Park Service, U.S. Fish and Wildlife Service, Plant Conservation Alliance, Mid-Atlantic Exotic Pest Plant Council (MAEPPC)

States listing *Albizia* as invasive: Alabama, Florida, Georgia, Kentucky, South Carolina, Tennessee, Texas, Virginia

*See page 16.

Amelanchier arborea
Downy Serviceberry

Say: am-meh-LANG-kee-er
  ar-BORE-ee-uh
Salt tolerance: Unknown
Size: 15–25 ft. tall/15–20 ft. wide
Origin: Eastern North America
Hardiness: USDA Zones 4–9
Family: Rosaceae (Rose)

Other names: Shadblow, Juneberry,
  shadbush, Sarvis-tree,
  serviceberry
Propagation: Seeds (after
  stratification)

Bill Cook

For best landscape effect, place them in front of a dark background to showcase their seasonal colors. They are also effective in woodland or naturalized gardens and along stream banks, ponds, and other wet areas.

There are several species of serviceberries. *Amelanchier canadensis* is often confused with *A. arborea* (downy serviceberry), and they are used interchangeably in the trade. Many of those sold in nurseries are *Amelanchier ×grandiflora* (apple serviceberry), a hybrid between *A. arborea* and *A. laevis* (Allegheny serviceberry).

White flowers two to four inches long are borne in pendulous clusters in early spring just before the leaves appear. Immediately following the flowers are small, round green berries, which turn red and then purple. These edible berries resemble blueberries and are delicious for eating or for making jams, jellies, and pies. Humans must beat the flocks of the birds and other wildlife if they are to get the berries.

Serviceberry may be a dense shrub with many small branches. However, with appropriate pruning, it can be shaped into a small tree. Fall colors are showy and range from yellow and orange to dull red.

Culture Serviceberry grows well in moist, well-drained, acid soil in full sun to part shade. However, it is tolerant of a wide range of soils, and tolerates pollution as well. Basal suckering may be a maintenance problem in urban plantings or in formal landscapes. If suckers are not removed, a shrubby growth habit will result. This can be used to advantage in naturalistic plantings or if the berries are harvested. Rusts, fireblight, fungi, mildews, sawflies, and other diseases and pests may infest serviceberries.

Arbutus unedo
Strawberry Tree

Say: ar-BYOO-tus YOO-nee-doe
Salt tolerance: Moderate
Size: 8–25 ft. tall/8–25 ft. wide
Origin: Southern Europe and the western Mediterranean region

Hardiness: USDA Zones 7–10
Family: Ericaceae (Heath)
Other names: Arbutus, cane apple
Propagation: Seeds; cuttings; layering

Arbutus is a slow-growing broadleaf evergreen which can be grown as a small tree or large shrub. Laurel-like foliage is dark green and glossy. In fall and winter the unusual fruits ripen in concert with a new crop of flowers.

fruits/flowers

Small, urn-shaped flowers resembling blueberry blossoms are white or pink and are produced in clusters of 10 to 30. Fruits are yellow, ripening to red, and have a rough, pebbled outer surface somewhat resembling a strawberry. Fruit is edible but not very tasty; however, it is popular with the avian population. Gray-brown bark exfoliates in thin plates to reveal the reddish young bark underneath. As the plant matures it becomes twisted and gnarled.

'Compacta' grows only six to ten feet tall and wide and has a distinctive contorted branching structure; 'Elfin King' bears flowers and fruits throughout the year and has a contorted, dwarf form; 'Rubra' has deep pink flowers but may be hard to find.

Use strawberry tree as a small specimen tree, or place it in a shrub border or woodland garden. Place away from walks and patios, where falling fruit can be a nuisance.

Culture Strawberry tree grows well in full sun or partial shade and on well-drained, acid soil. After establishment, it develops a long tap root and becomes very drought tolerant as well as wind resistant. The natural inclination of the plant is to grow into a formal rounded shape with multiple trunks. With considerable pruning, it can be trained as a single-trunked tree. Damage from pests and diseases is very rare.

Callistemon rigidus
Bottlebrush

Say: kal-lis-STEE-mon RIDGE-jid-us
Salt tolerance: Moderate
Size: 5–15 ft. tall/6–10 ft. wide
Origin: Australia
Hardiness: USDA Zones 8–11

Family: Myrtaceae (Myrtle)
Other names: Erect bottlebrush, stiff bottlebrush
Propagation: Seeds; cuttings

C. viminalis (weeping bottlebrush)

Bottlebrush is a stiff, upright, woody shrub to small tree. Showy spikes of flowers bloom on the ends of branches and beckon to nectar-feeding birds and insects. The actual flowers are very small and insignificant, but showy red filaments that project out from the tiny flowers make them spectacular when the tree is in full bloom. The flowers  encircle the stem to form the familiar bottlebrush shape, and foliage continues to grow beyond the ends of the flowers. Fruits are seed capsules clasped tightly around the stem that may remain on the plants for several years. Stiff, narrow leaves are fragrant in some species.

There are about 34 species of *Callistemon.* They range from small, prostrate to medium-sized shrubs, and a few grow to become medium-sized trees. Most popular in the South are *C. rigidus* (stiff bottlebrush) and *C. citrinus* (red or lemon bottlebrush). *C. rigidus* is the more hardy, if somewhat less showy, of the two. Flowers of stiff bottlebrush are not as wide and fuzzy as those of lemon bottlebrush, and the leaves are narrower and less fragrant. *Callistemon viminalis* (weeping bottlebrush) is a beautiful weeping form popular in southern Florida and California (Zones 9–11). Many cultivars have been selected from natural variants and many are hybrids between species.

Culture Provide full sun and well-drained soil for bottlebrush. Water regularly until well established, and then only during periods of drought. Regular fertilizer will maintain the deep green coloration of the leaves and keep them growing vigorously. Space so that there is room for air circulation around plants. Old, neglected shrubs can be pruned severely, if needed.

Cercis canadensis
Redbud

Say: SER-sis ka-na-DEN-sis
Salt tolerance: Slight to none
Size: 20–30 ft. tall/15–20 ft. wide
Origin: Eastern North America
Hardiness: USDA Zones 4–9
Family: Fabaceae (Pea)

Other name: Eastern redbud
Propagation: Seeds (collected in autumn and overwintered outdoors); cultivars usually grafted or started from cuttings

'Forest Pansy' (Zones 6–8) is a less drought-tolerant cultivar that has bright purple leaves in early spring. Flowers are a darker purple than the species. A cultivar named 'Alba' bears white flowers. 'Covey' has a weeping habit and 'Silver Cloud' sports green and white variegated foliage.

Texas redbud (*Cercis reniformis*) has outstanding glossy foliage in summer. Cultivars are available with pink or white flowers. 'Oklahoma' and 'Texas White' are superior cultivars.

Culture Care must be taken when the tree is planted to protect the bark, for it is very thin and easily damaged. Little or no fertilizer is needed, since, like other members of the pea family, it is able to fix nitrogen from the air.

Redbud prefers full sun to partial shade and rich, moist, well-drained soil. It will, however, tolerate drought and poor soil, but it is intolerant of wet sites. Sun in the early spring is desirable, but some protection from the hot summer sun is appreciated. Functional life of the redbud is no more than 10 to 20 years because of its vulnerability to urban stresses, diseases, and pests.

For two or three weeks in early spring, lavender, pealike flowers are prominently displayed on stems, branches, and even the trunks of redbuds. Following the flowers, broad, heart-shaped leaves emerge on the new growth of zigzag stems. The flattened pods that hang in clusters from the branches start out green and change to brown as they dry. Seedpods are persistent and often remain on the trees after leaves drop in the fall.

'Forest Pansy'

Chionanthus virginicus
Grancy Graybeard

Say: kye-oh-NAN-thus vir-JIN-ih-kus
Salt tolerance: Slight
Size: 15–30 ft. tall/8–20 ft. wide
Origin: Eastern United States
Hardiness: USDA Zones 3–9
Family: Oleaceae (Olive)
Other names: Fringetree, old man's beard

Propagation: Seeds (require three to five months of warmth for the roots to develop and then one or more months of chill—at least 41°F—for shoot formation)

In spring, white, honey-scented flowers cover grancy graybeard and perfume the area for about three weeks. Each blossom has four narrow, straplike petals about an inch long that dangle from threadlike stems in delicate, fleecy clusters six to eight inches long. Soft to the touch, these flowers quiver in the slightest breeze. This slow-growing, deciduous shrub or small tree has a spreading, rounded habit. Tolerant of air pollution and flowering at an early age, fringetree is a good choice for urban gardens.

Male trees put on a bigger show in spring because flowers have longer petals. However, the female bears fruit that is a good wildlife food. Dark blue, egg-shaped, half-inch-long fruits ripen in late summer.

Dwarf fringetree (*Chionanthus pygmaeus*), listed as endangered in Florida and by the U.S. Department of the Interior, is a dwarf form sometimes seen in the South. Blooms are just as beautiful as its larger cousin's, but the plants reach only three to four feet tall. The Chinese native (*C. retusus*) is perhaps a bit more showy than our native.

Culture Young container plants can be planted in the landscape anytime but have the greatest chance of success if planted in late fall through winter. Though best in slightly acid, fairly rich soil in open sun, they tolerate a wide range of conditions. For gardens with humus-starved soil, mulching generously with leaves, pine needles, or other organic material will be beneficial. Scale, spider mites, and a few diseases may be troublesome.

Cornus florida
Dogwood

Say: KOR-nus FLOR-id-uh
Salt tolerance: Moderate
Size: 25–30 ft. tall/25–30 ft. wide
Origin: Eastern and Southeastern United States

Hardiness: USDA Zones 5–9
Family: Cornaceae (Dogwood)
Other name: Flowering dogwood
Propagation: Cuttings; seeds

In spring the bracts (modified leaves that surround the inconspicuous true flower) of dogwoods light up woodlands, and the show continues through fall with colorful fruits and leaves. Healthy dogwoods usually stand up well to hurricane-force winds. Sizes vary with location and cultivar.

Flower bracts can be red, pink, or white, and they can be single or double. Berries are red or yellow, and leaves turn red and purple in fall.

Many selections of flowering dogwood have been named. A cultivar called 'Weaver's White' has shown much promise in Florida and the Deep South. Discovered in Gainesville, Florida, this cultivar bears whiter bracts than the species. Many cultivars are available, but gardeners in Zones 8 and 9 are advised to leave the pink- and red-flowering cultivars for gardeners farther north.

Although not available in Florida, other Southern states may have success with the Stellar Series, which are crosses between *Cornus florida* and *C. kousa.* More new hybrids that are crosses between *Cornus kousa* (kousa dogwood) and *C. nuttallii* (Pacific dogwood) have been released. Cultivars 'Venus' and 'Starlight' grow to 30 feet or more. *Cornus foemina* (swamp dogwood) is a good selection for wet sites.

Culture The dogwood is an understory tree, so plant it in partial or broken shade like that found underneath tall pines. Provide an acid, well-drained soil with plenty of organic matter. Mulch to maintain cool, moist soil, and provide plenty of space around the tree to promote good air circulation. Water regularly during the establishment period, and do not allow the trees to become extremely dry at any time. Because it is very shallow- rooted, it is intolerant of over-fertilization. Several problems beset the dogwood, including dogwood anthracnose, powdery mildew, flower and leaf blights, and other diseases. Avoiding stress and providing for the cultural needs of this plant are the best defenses against these maladies.

Cornus kousa

Kousa Dogwood

Say: KOR-nus KOO-suh
Salt tolerance: Moderate
Size: 15–20 ft. tall/15–20 ft. wide
Origin: Korea, Japan, China
Hardiness: USDA Zones 5–8
Family: Cornaceae (Dogwood)

Other name: Japanese flowering dogwood
Propagation: Seeds; rooted cuttings; cultivar cuttings grafted onto seedling rootstock

Todd Boland

light brownish-gray trunks mottled by smooth, cream to gray blotches. Leaves turn reddish-purple to scarlet in the fall.

In youth kousa dogwood is upright and vase-shaped, but with maturity it displays a more rounded form with a distinctive horizontal branching pattern. Many cultivars are available, and more are added every year. This tree offers multiseason interest with early summer, long-lasting flowers, autumn fruits, excellent summer foliage with occasional fall color, and interesting bark in winter.

Like the flowering dogwood (*Cornus florida*) the bracts (modified leaves) are more showy than the actual flowers, which are borne in inconspicuous yellow clusters nestled at the center of the bracts. The four white bracts are tapered at the tips and are one to two inches long. Flowers are produced after the leaves appear, and they extend the dogwood season by blooming two or three weeks later than *C. florida.*

The edible fruit is one-half to one inch in diameter. As the season progresses, the raspberry-like fruit turns from green to pink and then dull red. Bark on mature specimens is attractive, with

Culture Kousa dogwood prefers sun to partial shade and moist but well-drained acid soil. The tree is not particularly heat or drought tolerant, so irrigation during periods of drought and protection from hot, reflected sun is beneficial. Allow mulch or leaf litter to accumulate over the roots. No major pests are of concern, although borers sometimes attack. Kousa dogwood is resistant to anthracnose.

Dow Gardens

Cotinus coggygria
European Smoketree

Say: ko-TYE-nus kog-GY-gree-uh)
Salt tolerance: Moderate
Size: 10–15 ft. tall/8–14 ft. wide
Origin: Southern Europe and China
Hardiness: USDA Zones 4–8
Family: Anacardiaceae (Cashew)

Other names: Smoketree, smokebush, wig-tree
Propagation: Cuttings (very difficult on cultivars); seeds

Dow Gardens

Proven Winners

Several cultivars are available, many of which have been selected for purple flowers and foliage. 'Daydream' is a green-leaved selection that has dense blooms. 'Nordine' is a hardy form with purple leaves that hold their color well throughout the season. 'Royal Purple' and 'Velvet Cloak' are two commonly available selections with purple leaves. 'Grace' is a hybrid with the American smoketree (*C. obovatus*) that has purple leaves that mature to blue green. Other cultivars are also available.

Cotinus obovatus (American smoketree) is similar but is native to America. It grows 20 to 30 feet tall and has bluish to dark green leaves that turn brilliant colors in fall. It grows in much the same situations as its European cousin, but is very well adapted to limestone soil. Cultivars are available with red to purple leaves.

In early summer fuzzy clusters (panicles) of flowers about six inches long and wide bloom. The actual flowers are small and yellow-green. Plumelike filaments on the stems of the clusters make them showy. Panicles change colors as they age and at their peak cover the plant in smoky pink. Fall color can be excellent, with leaves turning from yellow to orange and then to brilliant red and purple. Multiple trunks are black and handsome.

Culture Place smoketree in full sun. Adaptable to adverse conditions, it can tolerate wet soil or hot, dry, gravelly soil, and it grows well in either alkaline or acid soil. A fibrous root system makes it easy to transplant. Both male and female plants are necessary for seed production.

Crataegus lacrimata
Pensacola Hawthorn

Say: krah-TEE-gus lah-crim-AY-tuh
Salt tolerance: Unknown
Size: 12–15 ft. tall/10–12 ft. wide
Origin: Western Florida Panhandle
Hardiness: USDA Zones 7–9
Family: Rosaceae (Rose)

Other names: Weeping haw, sandhill haw, yellow haw, Pensacola haw
Propagation: Cuttings of hardwood stems; layering; seeds (with stratification)

Hawthorns in general are the larval food plant for a few Lepidoptera species. They are important honey plants, and their dense, thorny branches provide cover and safe nest sites for birds. The berries are used as food by birds and mammals.

Cousins of the Pensacola haw, *Crataegus opaca* and *C. aestivalis*, often called mayhaw, have edible fruits that are used to make a tasty jelly. *Crataegus* is a very large genus, and several other species grow well in the South, including but not limited to *C. spathulata* (red haw), *C. marshallii* (parsley haw), *C. crusgalli* (cockspur haw), *C. floridana* (Florida haw), *C. uniflora* (dwarf haw), and *C. flava* (yellow-leaf haw). *Crataegus lacrimata* is not listed as a species in the APG II 2003 system. Kurz & Godfrey (*Trees of Northern Florida*) treat it as a distinct species.

The Pensacola hawthorn is a small deciduous tree or large shrub that is very noticeable in spring when it is covered with bright green leaves and hundreds of small white flowers that contrast with the dark bark. The half-inch flowers are followed by small, dull orange or russet red fruits. Distinctive bark is dark gray and deeply furrowed on old trunks. The tree is armed with stout, short thorns, and the branches often exhibit an attractive weeping habit.

Culture Plant Pensacola haw in full sun and extremely well-drained soil. Water well until established, after which it is very drought tolerant. Although hard to transplant from the wild, it can be successfully transplanted if root-pruned one winter and transplanted the next.

Cyrilla racemiflora
Titi

Say: sir-RIL-uh ray-see-mih-FLOR-uh
Salt tolerance: Moderate to slight
Size: 10–30 ft. tall/6–15 ft. wide
Origin: Southeastern U.S. coastal plain, Central and South America
Hardiness: USDA Zones 6–10

Family: Cyrillaceae (Cyrilla)
Other names: Leatherwood, swamp cyrilla
Propagation: Seeds; tip or root cuttings

one species in the Cyrillaceae family, but others recognize *Cyrilla parviflora* and *C. arida.*

Cyrilla is browsed by white-tailed deer. Although bees use the nectar to make honey, it is associated with a deleterious condition in bees called "purple brood."

Black titi (*Cliftonia monophylla*) is sometimes confused with swamp cyrilla, but it blooms earlier and produces buckwheatlike fruit.

Cliftonia (black titi)

Cliftonia seed clusters

The titi is easy to recognize when it blooms in spring and early summer. Conspicuous fingers of creamy white flowers hang in clusters (racemes) from the twig tips. Clusters of fruits in two-celled capsules follow the flowers and persist into winter. Evergreen to semievergreen leaves are two to four inches long and about one inch wide, generally oblong, simple, and alternately arranged on the stem.

Many botanists recognize only

Culture Titi is a swamp lover but will perform satisfactorily in well-drained soil if it is well mulched and watered during periods of drought. It forms thickets but is fairly easy to keep in bounds with regular pruning. Mass titi in full sun locations, or use them as part of informal hedges, mixed borders, woodland screens, as a specimen, or in any wet, sunny spot. Individual specimens of the long-lived titi have been documented as being well over 100 years old.

Eriobotrya japonica
Loquat

Say: Er-ee-oh-BOT-ree-uh juh-PON-ih-kuh

Salt tolerance: Moderate

Size: 20–30 ft. tall/30–35 ft. wide

Origin: China and Japan

Hardiness: USDA Zones 8–10

Family: Rosaceae (Rose)

Other name: Japanese plum

Propagation: Seeds; grafted cuttings

fast-growing, loquats usually do not live more than 25 or 30 years.

Seedlings are usually numerous underneath established trees. In south and central Florida seedlings have escaped into the wild, so the tree is not recommended for those areas. Purchase a cultivar or grafted variety for consistent fruit quality. 'Champagne', 'Gold Nugget', 'MacBeth', and 'Thales' are popular cultivars. 'Variegata' is a selection that has white and pale green splashes on the leaves.

Loquat trees are a great addition to a floral designer's garden. Flowers are attractive to bees and pollinating insects, and fruits are eaten by a variety of wildlife. Fruits are delicious eaten raw or they can be dried or made into jellies, jams, and preserves.

Loquat is an evergreen tree that has large, deep green leaves that are distinctively textured on top and light green to rusty colored and fuzzy on back. In late fall and early winter, fuzzy, fragrant white flowers bloom and are followed by edible, brightly colored yellow to orange fruits. Fruits and flowers are destroyed by temperatures around 28°F, which prevents the formation of fruit in the northern parts of its hardiness zone. Although generally

Culture Grow loquat in full sun and well-drained soil. Give it plenty of space for air circulation. Although trees are drought tolerant once established, a good mulch and adequate moisture will help them thrive. Avoid growing near pears, pyracantha, and other plants susceptible to fire blight. Fertilize sparingly to avoid excessive tender growth that might be sensitive to this disease.

Fortunella margarita and *F. crassifolia*
Kumquat

Say: for-tun-NEL-uh mar-gar-EE-tuh
   and krass-ih-FOH-lee-uh
Salt tolerance: Slight
Size: 8–12 ft. tall/8–12 ft. wide
Origin: China
Hardiness: USDA Zones 8–10

Family: Rutaceae (Citrus)
Other name: None
Propagation: Grafted onto the
   rootstock of trifoliate orange or
   other hardy rootstock

Kumquats have been called "the little gems of the citrus family." Glossy evergreen leaves provide the perfect backdrop for sweetly fragrant white flowers, which are borne singly or up to four together in the leaf axils. Fruit can be harvested for several months during the winter and early spring.

Although there are several species of kumquat, the ones most frequently grown in the South are 'Nagami' (*Fortunella margarita*) and 'Meiwa' (*Fortunella crassifolia*). 'Meiwa' is reportedly best to eat fresh. Fruits are round and sweet, and they are borne over a long season. 'Nagami' fruits are oblong and about two inches long. They have sweet rinds and sour insides.

With their sweet peel and tart pulp, kumquats are delicious picked and eaten right off the tree. In addition, they make excellent marmalades, jellies, candies, and pickles. The unique flavor adds a pleasant addition to many desserts and salads and is tasty in pork, fish, poultry, and lamb dishes. Giant swallowtail butterflies use it for their larval food plant, but their survival rate is low.

Culture Kumquats prefer well-drained soil and full to partial sun. Plants are very drought tolerant, but extra water during the bloom period or when fruit is developing is beneficial. Fertilize as growth begins with a fertilizer formulated for citrus. Hardy to 10°F, they are one of the hardiest of the citrus group. Usually they are carefree and easy to maintain, but several pests may attack them, including mealy bugs, chewing insect pests, and various fruit flies. Control recommendations can be obtained at any extension office.

Franklinia alatamaha
Ben Franklin Tree

Say: frank-LIN-ee-uh uh-lah-tah-MAH-hah

Salt tolerance: Unknown

Size: 15–25 ft. tall/10–15 ft. wide

Origin: Georgia along the Altamaha River

Hardiness: USDA Zones 5–9

Family: Theaceae (Tea)

Other name: Franklinia

Propagation: Seeds; cuttings

Janet Carson

The Ben Franklin tree produces three-inch, camellia-like flowers from late summer until frost. Clusters of yellow stamens glow from the center of each pure white blossom. This multistemmed, deciduous tree has dark green leaves that turn orange and red in fall, sometimes accompanied by a few late flowers. Subtly striped branches and woody seed capsules that persist into the winter add interest. Young trees are somewhat pyramidal in form but become more rounded with age.

In 1770 or thereabout, John and William Bartram discovered a grove of unknown trees growing along the Altamaha River in Georgia. On a later trip, they gathered seeds to propagate at their garden in Philadelphia. All of today's trees come from the Bartrams' seeds, and the tree has never again been found growing in the wild.

Culture The Ben Franklin tree grows in sun to partial shade. It appreciates well-drained, rich, acid soil. The tree is only moderately drought tolerant, so supplemental irrigation during dry spells may be needed. About the only trouble that befalls this tree is root rot. The control is to plant in areas where this disease has not been present and to make sure that drainage is perfect. Do not plant where cotton has been grown. Plants do not transplant well due to their sparsely fibrous root system, and they are intolerant of urban conditions. Despite these challenges, many are willing to make an extra effort to grow it. Those lucky enough to have a thriving specimen will rejoice in its presence and remember that without the Bartrams they would not have been so privileged.

Janet Carson

leaves in fall

Halesia diptera
Two-Winged Silverbell

Say: HAYLZ-ee-uh DIP-ter-uh
Salt tolerance: None
Size: 20–30 ft. tall/20–30 ft. wide
Origin: South Carolina to Arkansas and Texas
Hardiness: USDA Zones 6–8

Family: Styracaceae (Styrax)
Other name: Snowdrop tree
Propagation: Stem or root cuttings; layering; seeds (double stratification required)

Carolina silverbell

Chris Evans

Two-winged silverbell is a small ornamental tree that may grow taller in the wild than it does in urban conditions. Growth habit is normally multitrunked, although single-trunked specimens may sometimes occur. White, pendulous, bell-shaped clusters of flowers dangle from leaf axils in spring. Fruits that follow the blossoms are about two inches long with two corky wings. Fall color ranges from chartreuse to yellow-brown and is not particularly outstanding.

    Halesia diptera var. *magniflora* has larger flowers than the species. *Halesia tetraptera,* syn. *H. carolina* (Carolina silverbell), has smaller flowers with fused petals and

exhibits more cold hardiness (Zones 4-8). Another form sometimes called *Halesia parviflora* (little silverbell) also occurs in nature, but it is not as showy during the flowering period as are the other silverbells.

Culture Two-winged silverbell prefers partial shade. Soil should be moist, well drained, acid, and organically rich. Placement underneath a deciduous canopy will provide the sun in winter that the tree needs to set plenty of flowers and also protect it from too much sun during the summer. Trees are intolerant of heat, drought, and poor soil. In nature they occur in hammocks, floodplains, and swamp margins. Allow them to grow in the landscape where leaf litter and mulch accumulate.

Steve Hurst

seeds

Hamamelis virginiana
Witch-Hazel

Say: ham-uh-MEE-liss ver-jin-ee-AY-nuh
Salt tolerance: None
Size: 20–30 ft. tall/15–25 ft. wide
Origin: Eastern half of the United States plus Texas and Oklahoma
Hardiness: USDA Zones 4–8

Family: Hamamelidaceae (Witch-hazel)
Other name: None
Propagation: Seeds (after stratification)

Chris Evans

Chris Evans

at the same time the blooms are produced. However, the flowers, which look somewhat like yellow spiders attached to the tree, are more prominent after the leaves fall. The flowers are followed by oval-shaped, half-inch fruits which persist on the tree for about a year. When ripe, they explode and spread seeds up to 30 feet in all directions. Bark is smooth and light brown, but rough, scaly patches develop as the tree ages.

Two botanical varieties found in nature are *H. virginiana* var. *virginiana* and *H. virginiana* var. *parvifolia*. A cultivar called 'Rubescens' has reddish flowers. A few other species can be found, as well. *Hamamelis vernalis* (vernal witch-hazel) is a low shrub that is found in the Ozarks. Two Oriental species, *H. mollis* from China and *H. japonica* from Japan, have been crossed to produce *Hamamelis ×intermedia*. Many cultivars of this hybrid are in the trade.

Witch-hazel is a deciduous small tree or large shrub with spreading branches that form an irregular, rounded, open crown. Fragrant flowers with straplike, yellow petals bloom in late fall to early winter. Leaves turn yellow in fall, sometimes

Culture Witch-hazel occurs naturally along shady stream banks, but in cultivation it performs well in full sun or partial shade in light, moist soil. Pruning to remove lower branches and suckers that form around the base will be necessary if a tree form with multiple stems is desired.

Hovenia dulcis

Japanese Raisin Tree

Say: hoe-VEE-nee-ah DULL-sis
Salt tolerance: Unknown
Size: 30–35+ ft. tall/15–20 ft. wide
Origin: Japan, China, Korea
Hardiness: USDA Zones 6–10A

Family: Rhamnaceae (Buckthorn)
Other name: Honey tree
Propagation: Seeds; cuttings

J.S. Peterson

Japanese raisin tree is a small to medium-sized deciduous tree. Clusters of fragrant, greenish-white flowers bloom from the branch tips in early summer. Each flower is less than a half-inch in diameter. However, they are visually prominent because many tiny flowers bloom in clusters that are two to three inches wide. Glossy four- to six-inch-long leaves create light shade beneath the trees. Fall color is insignificant, and the leaves fall to the ground while they are still green.

Blossoms are followed by fleshy clusters of half-inch-diameter edible fruits, which ripen to reddish-brown, getting darker as they mature. Showy bark is light gray, and with age it becomes furrowed and peels in strips to reveal darker brown tones underneath.

This tree seems a good candidate for a specimen since it has an upright trunk. Branches hang down gracefully, and some nearly touch the ground if not pruned. Fruit is sweet and fragrant and can be eaten raw or cooked. Dried fruits, which resemble raisins and taste much like overripe apples or sweet raisins, are used for making wine and candy. The fine, hard wood is used in the construction of buildings and fine furniture.

Audrey Swindal

fruits

Culture Japanese raisin tree is tolerant of almost any soil as long as it is well drained. Full sun or partial shade suits it well. Bark is an outstanding feature, so lower branches can be removed to expose the trunk. Because the tree self-sows freely, many volunteer seedlings are likely to come up. Stems, fruits, and leaves can be a litter problem if the tree is near a walkway or patio.

Caution*

Koelreuteria paniculata

Golden Rain Tree

Say: keel-roo-TER-ee-uh pan-ick-yoo-LAY-tuh
Salt tolerance: Moderate
Size: 30–40 ft. tall/30–40 ft. wide
Origin: China, Japan, Korea

Hardiness: USDA Zones 5–9
Family: Sapindaceae (Soapberry)
Other name: Varnish tree
Propagation: Root cuttings; seeds

Jim Hawk

J.S. Peterson

Golden rain tree is a sparsely branched, medium-sized tree with a rounded outline. In summer it bears large clusters (panicles) of yellow, half-inch flowers for about two weeks. Flowers are followed by Chinese lanternlike seed pods which start out light green and change to apricot and then brown. Inside each "lantern" are hard, quarter-inch black fruits. Compound leaves about a foot long have 7 to 15 leaflets, which are coarsely and irregularly toothed. Newly emerged leaves have a wine or bronze cast; mature foliage is bright or dark green; and fall foliage, though inconsistent, is sometimes yellow or golden.

Blossoms fall beneath the golden rain tree, covering the ground with a golden carpet. Many seeds are produced, and they germinate readily, causing hundreds of seedlings to sprout up around a mature tree. Because of its aggressive tendencies, it has naturalized in many parts of the country and is invasive in some states. Golden rain tree is weak-wooded and limbs break easily in wind events.

Cultivars available include 'Rose Lantern' with pinkish seed pods, 'Fastigiata', and 'September', which blooms later than the species.

seed clusters
Jim Hawk

Culture Provide full sun and moist, well-drained soil for golden rain tree. The tree grows best in neutral to slightly alkaline soil, but it tolerates slightly acid soil, as well. It is tolerant of heat, drought, wind, air pollution, and general urban stressors.

*See page 16.

Lagerstroemia indica
Crape Myrtle

Say: la-ger-STREEM-ee-uh IN-dih-kuh
Salt tolerance: Slight to none
Size: 1.5–30+ ft. tall/1.5–20 ft. wide
Origin: China and Korea
Hardiness: USDA Zones 7–9A

Family: Lythraceae (Loosestrife)
Other names: None
Propagation: Softwood, semihardwood, hardwood, or root cuttings; seeds

leaves in fall

Crape myrtles range in size from 18 inches to more than 30 feet tall. During the summer, colorful panicles of hundreds of crepelike, crinkled flowers in shades of red, pink, lavender, purple, or white bloom in clusters on the tips of branches. Forms are mounding, rounded, vase-shaped, or upright and spreading. Bark color ranges from nondescript tan to light or dark brown, beige, orange, cinnamon, gray, pinkish-cream or whitish-beige. In many specimens the bark exfoliates to reveal new bark in various shades of color. Autumn brings another show when the leaves turn brilliant hues.

Breeding programs have produced cultivars that show increased tolerance to powdery mildew, which so often plagues many of the older types.

Crape myrtle has a naturally fascinating form that severe pruning destroys. On tree crape myrtles, remove branches that are crossing or rubbing against each other and shoots growing into the center of the canopy. Cut back to a side branch or close to the trunk. Remove basal sprouts as needed. Prune during the winter before spring growth. Tip pruning following a flush of flowers will sometimes stimulate another flush, but this practice is impractical and unnecessary on mature, low-maintenance trees.

Culture Plant in well-drained soil and full sun in an area that offers good air circulation. Crape myrtle is very drought tolerant, but newly planted trees should be watered regularly until they are well established. A light sprinkling of balanced fertilizer around young plants during the growing season will stimulate growth. Mulch with organic mulch such as pine needles or hardwood chips.

Magnolia ashei
Ashe Magnolia

Say: mag-NO-lee-uh ASH-ee-eye
Salt tolerance: Unknown
Size: 10–20 ft. tall/12–15 ft. wide
Origin: Western Florida Panhandle
    eastward to about Leon County

Hardiness: USDA Zones 6–9
Family: Magnoliaceae (Magnolia)
Other name: Bigleaf magnolia
Propagation: Seeds; layering;
    cuttings

at the base of the other three petals.

This magnolia is a deciduous shrub or small understory tree. It can be distinguished from all other trees and shrubs by the huge leaves with eared, or cordate, bases. Blooms may appear when the tree is three to four years old. The fruit is a cone-shaped pod containing large red seeds.

This magnolia may be listed as *Magnolia macrophylla* subsp. *ashei*. It differs from *M. macrophylla* because it is smaller and often multitrunked with smaller leaves, fewer stamens and pistils, and smaller seeds.

The Ashe magnolia is hard to miss in the woods or in the landscape. Very large leaves from 18 to 30

inches long with wavy edges and "ear lobes" at the base are distinctive. On top, leaves are bright green and shiny, but on the bottom they are chalky white. In spring, creamy white flowers up to 12 inches wide appear at the same time as the leaves. The six-petaled flowers have purple blotches at the base of three of the petals, and less conspicuous purple blotches may be

Culture The Ashe magnolia requires partial shade and moist, well-drained soil. Shelter trees from strong winds to avoid shredding the papery leaves and breaking the brittle branches. Never remove this tree from the wild. Not only does it transplant poorly, but it is listed as endangered by the Florida Department of Agriculture. Sometimes young, container-grown trees can be found at nurseries that sell rare or native plants. Unless their cultural requirements are rigidly observed, the trees may be short-lived.

Magnolia grandiflora
Southern Magnolia

Say: mag-NO-lee-uh gran-dih-FLOR-uh
Salt tolerance: Moderate
Size: Varies with cultivar
Origin: Southeastern United States
Hardiness: USDA Zones 6–10

Family: Magnoliaceae (Magnolia)
Other names: Bull bay, magnolia
Propagation: Cultivars grafted onto seedlings of the species; cuttings

Beauty' has smaller flowers that are five to six inches across, and it grows to 30 feet tall and spreads 10 to 15 feet wide. Other compact forms are 'Alta' and 'Hasse'.

One of the most popular cultivars is 'Little Gem'. This beauty has lustrous, dark green leaves that are bronze to brown underneath. Flowers three to five inches in diameter begin blooming at an early age, and it grows 20 to 40 feet tall and 12 feet wide.

On a mature and well-grown magnolia, wide branches sweep the ground in a circle 30 to 50 feet wide, and from there they form a pyramid-shaped silhouette that rises 60 to 80 or more feet into the air. A profusion of fragrant white flowers up to 12 inches in diameter bloom in spring and sporadically throughout the season. Fruits are red, kidney-shaped seeds that hang by threads from a reddish-brown, conelike structure.

Many cultivars of magnolia are available. Homeowners can choose a tree that grows large if room allows, or a small cultivar can be selected if space is limited. 'Majestic Beauty' forms a large tree of pyramidal form, grows 30 to 50 feet tall, and spreads to about 20 feet. 'Bracken's Brown

Culture Plant magnolia in either sun or shade. It prefers rich, well-drained soil but is tolerant of a wide range of soils. Once established it is quite drought tolerant. Since roots are very near the surface and the shade is very dense, it is competitive for water and nutrients. Only a few groundcovers can survive beneath it.

Magnolia ×soulangeana
Saucer Magnolia

Say: mag-NOL-yuh × soo-lan-jee-AY-nuh

Salt tolerance: Slight to none
Size: 20–30 ft. tall/15–25 ft. wide
Origin: China
Hardiness: USDA Zones 5–9A
Family: Magnoliaceae (Magnolia)

Other names: Tulip tree, cup magnolia

Propagation: Cuttings of terminal buds in summer (if exact duplicates are wanted); seeds stratified three to six months in refrigerator (may vary from original)

Culture Saucer magnolias like full sun or very light shade and moist, fertile, well-drained, acid soil. Shallow roots make them susceptible to extended drought, so they should be mulched well and watered if rainfall is insufficient. Fertilize in spring just as new growth emerges with general, all-purpose fertilizer. Problems may include magnolia scale and the sooty mold that accompanies it. Sapsuckers may injure the bark.

Saucer magnolia starts out as a multistemmed large shrub and typically grows into a low-branched tree. Growth rate is medium, a newly planted specimen growing from 10 to 15 feet over a ten-year period. Branches spread almost as wide as the tree is tall, and at maturity the crown is pyramidal to rounded in outline. The trees are grown for their showy flowers that bloom in late winter before the leaves appear. Sometimes a late freeze (25 to 28°F) kills the flowers that are in bloom.

Saucer magnolia tends to produce multiple stems, but they can be pruned to favor one dominant trunk. Do this pruning while the tree is young. If pruning is necessary to shape the crown, it should be done as soon as flowering is over.

Many cultivars of saucer magnolia are available, and new cultivars appear with regularity. They are available with flowers of many colors, including all shades of white, pink, and purple, as well as yellow.

Magnolia stellata
Star Magnolia

Say: mag-NO-lee-uh stell-AY-tuh
Salt tolerance: Unknown
Size: 15–20 ft. tall/10–15 ft. wide
Origin: Japan

Hardiness: USDA Zones 4–9
Family: Magnoliaceae (Magnolia)
Other name: Japanese star magnolia
Propagation: Cuttings; seeds

color is not exceptional. Noticeable in the winter landscape are the fuzzy terminal pussy willowlike buds held on the glossy brown stems of young twigs. The main trunk is silvery gray.

Remaining compact for many years, the star magnolia is a good selection for small properties. It blooms at an early age, and flowers are lightly fragrant. Several cultivars are available and include 'Royal Star' (double-flowering form); 'Rosea' (light pink flowers fading to white); 'Rubra' (purplish-rose flowers that fade to pink); 'Centennial' (large, many-petaled flowers with a tint of pink on the outside); and 'Waterlily' (larger flowers with narrower but more abundant petals than others).

Star magnolia can be grown as a large shrub or small tree. Form is upright and oval in youth, but with age it becomes more spreading and mounding. The oblong leaves are about four inches long and one and one-half inches wide. In late winter to early spring, snowy white, star-shaped flowers with 12 to 30 delicate petals appear before the leaves.

Blossoms are followed by reddish-green knobby aggregate fruits which are about two inches long. Slits open in mature fruits to reveal brilliant red seeds. Newly emerging leaves have a bronze cast but quickly turn dark green. In fall the leaves turn yellow to bronze but

Culture Star magnolia prefers morning sun with filtered shade during the hottest part of the day. It appreciates evenly moist, acid, well-drained soil but is adaptable to a wide range of soils and is pollution tolerant. Thick, fleshy roots grow near the surface and resent disturbance. Blooms are frequently injured by early spring frosts, so plant them in the coolest area of the landscape to delay flowering. However, protect them from heavy ice or snow that can break the soft wood. Magnolia scale may be problematic but can be controlled with horticultural oil.

Malus angustifolia
Southern Crabapple

Say: MAL-us an-gus-tee-FOH-lee-uh
Salt tolerance: None
Size: 15–25 ft. tall/15–25 ft. wide
Origin: Southern United States
Hardiness: USDA Zones 5–8

Family: Rosaceae (Rose)
Other name: Crabapple
Propagation: Whip grafts; budding; softwood cuttings; removal of suckers.

requirements for flower and fruit set are low, and the deep red fruit is highly ornamental. An extension office can help determine the most dependable crabapples for particular parts of the South.

Pink buds of the crabapple open to reveal extremely fragrant white to pink flowers about one inch wide. Flowers occur in clusters of three to five. Small, edible, yellowish-green rounded fruits about an inch in diameter can be canned, made into jellies, or left on the tree for birds and other wildlife. Blunt-tipped leaves have wavy, sawtoothed edges and are dull green above and pale green below.

Southern crabapple is rarely sold at nurseries, but many cultivars and hybrids have been documented and more are being developed each year. 'Callaway' shows excellent disease resistance to most crabapple diseases and is highly recommended for Southern gardens. Chill

Culture Crabapple needs full sun and well-drained, moist, acid soil. Prune to remove sucker growth, to remove undesirable branches and shape the tree, and to open it up to light and air. Maintain a distance of at least 500 feet from red cedar (*Juniperus virginiana*) to prevent the spread of cedar apple rust. Although moderately drought tolerant, trees should be watered during periods of drought to keep them from becoming stressed. Many diseases, including apple scab, fireblight, rusts, leaf spot, and powdery mildew, affect crabapples. Insect pests may include tent caterpillars, aphids, Japanese beetle, borers, spider mites, and scale.

Caution*

Parkinsonia aculeata

Jerusalem Thorn

Say: PAR-kin-SO-nee-uh ah-kew-lee-AY-tuh

Salt tolerance: High

Size: 15–20 ft. tall/20–25 ft. wide

Origin: West Indies and South America; naturalized throughout southern United States

Hardiness: USDA Zones 8–11

Family: Fabaceae (Bean)

Other names: Mexican paloverde, jellybean tree

Propagation: Seeds

Because of its small size and graceful form, Jerusalem thorn is often chosen for suburban landscapes. Light shade allows for turf underneath, and it is attractive during its early years.

seeds

Jerusalem thorn is a deciduous to semideciduous small, spiny tree with attractive, fernlike foliage and a graceful, drooping form. Showy pealike flowers bloom sporadically but with greatest abundance in spring and summer. The yellow flowers are borne in clusters (racemes) and have five petals, the largest of which turns orange with age. Fruit, which ripens in late summer, is a sharp-pointed tan pod two to four inches long. The tree has long, straight spines, which occur in pairs at the bases of leaves. The trunk is initially green but becomes gray and woody with age.

This tree naturalizes aggressively and is considered a noxious weed in many parts of the world. It is invasive in Australia, Africa, Hawaii, and other islands in the Pacific Ocean, and some report that it has escaped cultivation along the Gulf coast.

Culture Full sun is preferred, but light-filtered shade is also acceptable. The Jerusalem thorn is adaptable to almost any soil as long as it is well drained. Both drought and heat tolerant, it should do well on natural rainfall. Because of its high tolerance to salt, it is sometimes chosen for seaside plantings. Protect from mechanical injury, as the bark is thin and easily damaged. Bark damage could shorten the already brief 15- to 20-year life expectancy.

*See page 16.

44

Pinckneya bracteata
Fevertree

Say: PINK-nee-uh brak-tee-AY-tuh
Salt tolerance: None
Size: 15–20 ft. tall/12–18 ft. wide
Origin: Georgia, Florida, and South
    Carolina
Hardiness: USDA Zones 7B–9

Family: Rubiaceae (Madder)
Other names: Georgia fevertree,
    pinckneya, fever-bark tree,
    Georgia fever-bark
Propagation: Seeds; removal of
    suckers; cuttings

Gil Nelson

has been historically brewed into a tea and used for reducing fever.

The tree is critically imperiled in South Carolina and vulnerable in certain Georgia counties, according to NatureServe, and it is on the Florida list of threatened plants.

Jeff McMillan

Fevertree is quite showy in late spring to early summer, when clusters of yellowish-green flowers bloom. The tubular blossoms are about one inch long and have five petals that curl back on themselves at the tips. However, it is not the flowers but the cream to bright rose-colored petal-like sepals that demand attention. At least one of the five sepals expands into a leaflike white, pink, or rose bract that dangles in the breeze. The deciduous tree has large, dark green leaves from five to eight inches long and three to four inches wide. Round, brown-spotted seed capsules follow the blossoms and persist throughout the winter.

Pinckneya is rare and may be difficult to obtain. Wild specimens often spread by producing root suckers. The bitter bark of the plant

Culture In nature, fevertree grows in poorly drained places such as in and at the margins of streamheads, bayheads, and seepage swamps. In landscapes it must be placed in an area where it is irrigated regularly, as it is not drought tolerant. It requires acid, moisture-retentive soil. Flowering is best in full sun, but the tree grows in partial sun, as well. Root rot is problematic. Mulch to maintain a cool root zone. Gardeners in zones 7A and lower may have success growing fevertree in a container and moving it to a protected place in the winter.

45

Prunus angustifolia
Chickasaw Plum

Say: PROO-nus an-gus-tee-FOH-lee-uh
Salt tolerance: Moderate
Size: 12–20 ft. tall/15–20 ft. wide
Origin: Southern United States
Hardiness: USDA Zones 6–9

Family: Rosaceae (Rose)
Other name: Sand plum
Propagation: Seeds; division of
  suckers

Chris Evans

(American plum) and *P. umbellata* (flatwoods plum). Tasty preserves and jellies are made from the fruits. Plants provide excellent cover and food for birds and other wildlife, and bees and butterflies gather pollen and nectar. Floral designers enjoy forcing the branches into flower for their designs.

The Chickasaw plum is a deciduous shrub or small tree that springs up in disturbed places throughout the South. In early spring, small, half-inch flowers with five white petals and reddish-tipped anthers clothe the Chickasaw plum so that a mass of white is all that can be seen from a distance. Flowers are followed by one-half- to one-inch fruits that are bright yellow to red and may be round to oval. The fruit is juicy and ripens in late summer. Most often the trees grow in dense thickets.

Closely related and having similar uses are *P. americana*

Culture Chickasaw plum is easily grown in average, well-drained, acid soil in full sun to partial shade. Well-established trees are very drought tolerant. Prune to improve form, if needed. Remove root suckers to prevent any unwanted spread, or if there is room, allow them to colonize. Insects and diseases are not usually a problem, but tent caterpillars may need to be controlled. No spraying is necessary to produce fruit that is free of worms. Trees are often literally loaded with fruits, producing as much as two bushels on mature plants.

Prunus cerasoides var. *campanulata*
Taiwan Cherry

Say: PROO-nus seer-rah-SOY-deez
variety kam-pan-yoo-LAY-tuh
Salt tolerance: Unknown
Size: 15–25 ft. tall/15–25 ft. wide
Origin: China, Taiwan, Japan's Ryukyu
Islands
Hardiness: USDA Zones 7B–9

Family: Rosaceae (Rose)
Other names: Bell-flowered cherry,
Formosan cherry
Propagation: Seeds after cold
treatment; tip cuttings taken in
spring

Taiwan cherry produces a profusion of deep rosy pink, bell-shaped flowers in early spring.

Kwanzan

cerasoides var. *campanulata*. Yoshino cherry (*Prunus xyedoensis*) (Zones 5B–8A) is the beautiful flowering cherry that brightens the spring in the Washington, D.C., Tidal Basin. Kwanzan cherry (*Prunus serrulata*) (Zones 5B–9A) is another popular species that is frequently grown. The cherry trees are generally short lived, seldom lasting more than 10 to 15 years.

Flowers appear before the leaves and are borne in clusters of two to six. Following the flowers, small green cherries (about one-half inch in diameter or less) turn red and then black. Fall foliage can be bronzy-red to orange. Flowering begins as early as late January in Florida.

'Okame', one of the most popular cultivars of Taiwan cherry, is a cross between *Prunus incisa* and *P.*

Culture Taiwan cherry is best in full sun in its northern range, but some protection from sun is appreciated in its southernmost range. It appreciates regular watering. Pruning to thin out the canopy and allow light to penetrate the interior foliage will result in a pleasing specimen. Branches with an upright orientation should be removed and those with a wider angle should be encouraged.

Leaf spot, twig canker, and black knot are disease problems that might be troublesome. Certain worms, aphids, borers, spider mites, and scales of several types may infest cherries. Treat if necessary, and keep trees healthy with regular applications of fertilizer.

Pyrus calleryana 'Bradford'
Bradford Pear

Say: PIE-rus kal-ler-ee-AY-nuh
Salt tolerance: Moderate
Size: 30–50 ft tall/20–30 ft. wide
Origin: Korea and China
Hardiness: USDA Zones 5A–9A

Family: Rosaceae (Rose)
Other names: Callery pear, ornamental pear
Propagation: Tip cuttings; grafting; seeds (avoid; not true to type)

Leaves in fall

Unfortunately, the Bradford pear has a few serious flaws. The combination of vigorous growth, weak wood, and poor branch structure has been its undoing. Branches are attached to the trunk at too narrow an angle, and as the branches grow in girth, the tree literally pushes itself apart. The first strong wind or ice storm will cause the tree to break up.

Although the spring flowers are quite beautiful, their odor is unpleasant to some people. Small, inedible fruits can be messy in the landscape. Seedlings sometimes come up underneath established trees. They are not like the parent, however. Thickets of thorny escapees may form monocultures that exclude native species. Named cultivars must be propagated from tip cuttings or grafted onto seedlings of the species.

In spring the Bradford pear sports showy white flowers, which appear before the leaves. Fall color is dazzling, ranging from red and orange to dark maroon. Fruits are attractive to a number of bird species as well as to squirrels and other small animals.

Culture Mulch with organic mulch out to the dripline of the tree, but do not allow the mulch to touch the trunk. Choose a strong tree with a single leader and prune while young to eliminate branches that join the trunk at sharp angles. Fertilize very scantily, if at all, since fertilizer will further encourage its naturally fast, weak growth. Plan to replace the tree in about 15 years, if it lasts that long.

Stewartia malacodendron
Silky Camellia

Say: stew-ART-ee-uh mah-lah-koh-
   DEN-dron
Salt tolerance: Unknown
Size: 10–15 ft. tall/10–15 ft. wide
Origin: Southern United States

Hardiness: USDA Zones 7–9
Family: Theaceae (Tea)
Other name: Virginia stewartia
Propagation: Cuttings; seeds
   (difficult)

Edmund R. Taylor

Stewartia ovata (mountain stewartia) is also native to the South. Flowers are about three inches wide and are white with whitish to purple filaments. Each petal is crimped and crenulated. *Stewartia monadelpha* (tall stewartia) is a good choice for Southern gardens since it displays a great deal of heat tolerance. *Stewartia pseudocamellia* (Japanese stewartia) is an excellent choice for Zones 5B–7.

James Henderson

Silky camellia is a multibranched deciduous large shrub or small tree with branches that tend to grow horizontally, forming a pagoda-like arrangement. White, waxy flowers, which appear in midsummer, have dark purple filaments and bluish anthers. Bark is gray-brown, and the fruit is a woody, egg-shaped capsule containing five valves and wingless, lustrous brown seeds.

Silky camellia can be found as an understory plant in rich, wooded bluffs, ravine slopes, and creek banks in scattered localities in the South. It is uncommon throughout its range. Although it is hard to propagate and establish, it is one of the South's most beautiful native trees.

Culture High shade, early morning sun, and well-drained soil are preferred by this native tree. It is finicky as far as site is concerned, so every effort should be made to place it in a location to its liking. Plants have a slow growth rate and are difficult to transplant and to propagate.

Vaccinium arboreum
Sparkleberry

Say: vak-SIN-ee-um ar-BOR-ee-um
Salt tolerance: Slight
Size: 6–30 ft. tall/4–15 ft. wide
Origin: Southeastern United States
Hardiness: USDA Zones 6–9

Family: Ericaceae (Heath)
Other names: Farkleberry, tree huckleberry
Propagation: Cuttings (hard to root); seeds

Culture Sparkleberry prefers full sun to partial shade and moist, acid soil, but it can adapt to a wide range of soils, including alkaline. It can be found growing on sand dunes; hammocks; dry, sterile hillsides; in rocky woods; and in abandoned fields and meadows. However, it also occurs on moist sites such as wet bottomlands and along creek banks. Hardly a situation exists where sparkleberry will not grow satisfactorily.

Sparkleberry is North America's largest blueberry. This small deciduous tree or large shrub has flaking reddish bark, a crooked trunk, and contorted branches. Kinship to the blueberry family is evidenced by flowers that hang down from the stems in typical blueberry fashion. Black, persistent, quarter-inch berries are attractive to wildlife but not very tasty for humans.

Sparkleberry is important to wildlife. White-tailed deer browse them in many areas, and several species of hares and rabbits feed on the leaves and twigs. Fruits and flowers provide spring and summer food for bobwhite quail, black bear, and many species of birds. The flowers are attractive to various bees, and the leaves are the larval plant for Henry's elfin butterfly. Many butterflies enjoy nectar from the flowers.

Sparkleberry can be used as rootstock for some edible blueberries such as the highbush blueberry (*Vaccinium corymbosum*). The resulting cultivars are well suited to droughty upland sites with soils that have a relatively high pH. This allows people who could not ordinarily grow blueberries a better chance for success.

fruits

Vitex agnus-castus
Chaste Tree

Say: VY-teks AG-nus KAS-tus
Salt tolerance: High to moderate
Size: 15–20 ft. tall/15–20 ft. wide
Origin: Europe, Asia
Hardiness: USDA Zones 6–10

Family: Lamiaceae (Mint)
Other names: Monk's pepper, hemp tree, chasteberry
Propagation: Tip cuttings; seeds

In addition to the species with lilac flowers, cultivars such as 'Alba', 'Colonial Blue', 'Rosea', and 'Silver Spire' offer flowers of white, blue, or pink. *Vitex negundo* and *V. rotundifolia* are also used in landscapes, but they differ significantly from *Vitex agnus-castus*.

The chaste tree has had a multitude of interesting uses over the years. In Rome, virgins carried twigs of it as a symbol of chastity. Because of its peppery-tasting seeds and reported ability to quiet the sexual appetite, it has been called "monk's pepper." It has been used for treatment of female difficulties such as menstrual and menopausal disorders for at least 2,500 years.

Each spring, slender, spiked clusters (racemes) of fragrant, lavender flowers three to six inches long pierce the air from the ends of each branch. Following the flowers, a round, fleshy seed about one-eighth of an inch in diameter is produced.

Leaves are distinctive because each leaflet is attached to a common point with five to seven fingerlike leaflets (palmately compound). They are dark grayish-green on top and lighter and hairy underneath. When brushed against or bruised, they give off a sharp, aromatic scent.

Culture Chaste tree prefers full sun and moist, well-drained soil. It is, however, tolerant of drought, heat, and salt. Pruning off old blossoms may encourage another flush of flowers. It is easily pruned into a shrub, or it can be limbed up and grown as a small tree with multiple trunks. The trees are susceptible to damage from nematodes, but adding organic amendments to the soil can help to reduce the nematode population.

Chapter 2
Flowering Shrubs

The array of flowering shrubs that grow well in the South is mind-boggling. With so many species, hybrids, and cultivars, an almost infinite variety is available. Choose from among them for a variety of landscape purposes as well as for year-round beauty. Choose some for their attractiveness to butterflies, birds, and other wildlife. While many non-blooming evergreen or deciduous trees and shrubs may form the major backbone of the landscape, it is the flowering shrubs that add sparkle and pizzazz.

Bigleaf hydrangea blooms in this partially shaded Southern garden.

Japanese camellia adds color to the fall, winter, and spring garden.

Abelia ×grandiflora
Glossy Abelia

Say: a-BEE-lee-uh × gran-dih-FLOR-uh
Salt tolerance: Slight
Size: 3–10 ft. tall/3–6 ft. wide
Origin: Hybridized in Italy
Hardiness: USDA Zones 5–9

Family: Linnaeaceae (Twinflower)
Other name: Abelia
Propagation: Cuttings of hardwood
  stems; layering

Glossy abelia is an evergreen to semievergreen hybrid between *Abelia chinensis* and *A. uniflora*. It is a spreading, dense, rounded, multistemmed shrub with arching and cascading branches. Small, funnel-shaped, white flowers flushed with pink are borne in terminal clusters of three to five, and they bloom profusely for most of the summer. Persistent sepals are bronze to purplish in color and add to the coloration of the plant. Leaves are lustrous dark green, often tinged with red on top and a paler green underneath. In the southern portions of its range it is evergreen. Butterflies and hummingbirds are attracted to the flowers.

Low-growing selections exist that are better suited to small gardens. 'Francis Mason' grows three to four feet tall and has pink flowers and new leaves that are rich yellow. 'Prostrata' reaches about one and one-half to two feet tall, is more compact, and has smaller leaves that turn purple-green in winter. 'Sherwood' tops out at three to four feet tall with a bit wider spread. 'Edward Goucher' averages five by five feet at maturity and bears fragrant, clear pink flowers. 'Confetti' has cream-margined foliage that turns reddish in cool weather.

Culture Glossy abelia prefers full sun to partial shade and fairly rich, moist, well-drained, acid soil. It has no serious pests and is moderately drought tolerant. Hard pruning in late winter will rejuvenate old plants. If the natural fountain shape is wanted, old canes should be pruned from the center of the plant at ground level.

Acca sellowiana
Pineapple Guava

Say: AK-uh sel-lo-wee-AH-nuh
Salt tolerance: High
Size: Size: 8–30 ft. tall/8–30 ft. wide
Origin: Southern Brazil, Paraguay, Uruguay, Northern Argentina
Hardiness: USDA Zones 8–10
Family: Myrtaceae (Myrtle)

Other names: Feijoa, guavasteen
Propagation: Cuttings; named selections grafted onto seedling root stock; cuttings or grafts from known cultivars; seeds, but quality is unpredictable

and greenish-white, tasty pulp ripen in fall. Oval-shaped green leaves two to three inches long and silvery underneath give the plants a silvery sheen in the landscape.

Until recently, feijoa was known as *Feijoa sellowiana,* and it may still be found labeled as such at garden centers. Regardless of the scientific name, one should select cultivars for fruit quality and the ability to self-pollinate. The vegetatively propagated cultivar 'Coolidge' has produced well in Florida and shows promise for the South. Even the flower petals are edible and make a tasty addition to salads and other dishes.

Culture Full sun to part shade and well-drained, slightly acid to neutral soil are preferred. Plants are drought and salt tolerant and require very little fertilizer. They are amenable to pruning and can be shaped into shrubs or grown as small trees with the lower limbs removed.

Although pineapple guava is hardy to 10° F, it does best where the winters are cool and the summers moderate with temperatures that range from 80–90° F. Feijoas need 100–200 chilling hours below 45° F. Heat stress in the summer may cause them to drop fruit prematurely.

Pineapple guava is a slow-growing, evergreen shrub. In spring, unusual, fleshy-petaled flowers about one inch wide bloom. Each flower is purplish-red inside and white on the outside and is centered by a cluster of erect, showy red stamens with yellow-tipped anthers. Round or egg-shaped fruits with gray-green peels

Ardisia crenata
Coral Ardisia

Say: ar-DIZ-ee-uh kre-NAY-tuh
Salt tolerance: Moderate
Size: 2–6 ft. tall/2–3 ft. wide
Origin: Japan to N. India
Hardiness: USDA Zones 7–10

Family: Myrsinaceae (Myrsine)
Other names: Coralberry, Christmas berry, Hilo holly, marlberry, ardisia
Propagation: Seeds; volunteers

Coral ardisia has dark green, glossy leaves; white or pinkish flowers; and clusters of showy scarlet berries. One look at these attractive plants in full berry is enough to make most gardeners want to include them in their landscape. However, as gardeners learn to recognize exotic invasive species and become aware of their potential to harm natural areas, they are less likely to allow them in their gardens.

Ardisia escallonoides (marlberry) is native to Florida and does not have invasive tendencies like *A. crenata*. The red berries of coral ardisia are attractive to birds, particularly cedar waxwings and mockingbirds, which carry the seeds into natural areas. Seeds germinate readily, have a high rate of germination, and are viable for a long time.

Cutting coral ardisia down has little effect, as it resprouts vigorously after cutting. Burning will not eradicate the plant because the thick foliage does not carry fire well, and plants resprout quickly following a fire. Fruits are produced on plants within two years from the time they are planted as seeds. A mature plant is usually surrounded by a carpet of seedlings capable of displacing small native groundcovers such as violets and trilliums.

Coral ardisia is naturalized on two islands in Hawaii. In Florida and Louisiana it has invaded natural areas in several places, and it has been reported in Texas too, where it dominates the understory in parts of two reserves. In Florida coral ardisia is listed as a Category I exotic invasive that is capable of displacing native species. Gardeners in mild coastal areas of the South are discouraged from including this plant in their gardens.

Culture Coral ardisia prefers shade to partial shade and rich, deep, organic soil that is moist but well drained. Mulch will help maintain moisture and enrich the soil as it decomposes. Prune back to control height if desired. Ardisia is frozen to the ground by freezing temperatures.

* See page 16.

Berberis bealei
Leatherleaf Mahonia

Say: BUR-bur-iss BEEL-lee-eye
Salt tolerance: Moderate
Size: 4–6 ft. tall/3–4 ft. wide
Origin: China
Hardiness: USDA Zones 6B–9A

Family: Berberidaceae (Barberry)
Other name: Beale's barberry, Beale's mahonia
Propagation: Seeds; cuttings

This evergreen shrub has tough, leathery, compound leaves bearing nine to thirteen coarsely spined leaflets, which are borne in horizontal tiers up each unbranched stalk. Dense, three- to six-inch-long spikes of slightly fragrant yellow flowers begin blooming in January. They arise from the top of the plant and are held at a perfect height for viewing up close. Pendulous masses of bluish-purple fruits about the size of small grapes follow the flowers and are relished by birds, squirrels, and other wildlife. In fall

the plants take on a reddish color, and occasionally a solid red leaf will appear.

Leatherleaf mahonia is one of more than 70 species, and probably an equal number of hybrids and cultivars of mahonia exist worldwide. Creeping mahonia (*Berberis repens*) and Oregon grapeholly (*B. aquifolium*) are native to the Pacific Northwest. Chinese mahonia (*B. fortunei*) is frequently grown and lacks the sharp, stiff leaf spines of other species. Chinese hollygrape (*B. lomariifolia*) has long, narrow, prickly leaves.

Leatherleaf mahonia is invasive in parts of the Southeast. Check with authorities in your area before including this plant in your garden.

Culture Leatherleaf mahonia blooms best if a few hours of morning sun can be managed, but it cannot tolerate full sun. Moist but well-drained, slightly acid soil is preferred. Fertilize with a light sprinkling of complete fertilizer in late winter.

Sometimes old stems may grow six or more feet tall and become leggy and top heavy. The appearance can be improved by removing about one-third of the tallest canes at ground level. New stems will grow from the base.

fruit

* See page 16.

Buddleja davidii
Butterfly Bush

Say: BUD-lee-uh duh-VID-ee-eye
Salt tolerance: Slight
Size: 6–12 ft. tall/4–15 ft. wide
Origin: China and Japan
Hardiness: USDA Zones 5–10
Family: Scrophulariaceae (Figwort)

Other names: Buddleia (alternate spelling), summer lilac
Propagation: Easy from cuttings; seeds; seedlings from established plants

B. alternifolia
(fountain butterfly bush)

Phillip Oliver

Butterfly bush has showy four- to ten-inch-long, nodding clusters of fragrant flowers on long, arching canes. From midsummer until frost, flowers ranging in color from lilac to pink, red, purple, or white (most with orange centers) beckon to butterflies, moths, and other insects, as well as to hummingbirds. Lance-shaped leaves are gray-green to green above and white and fuzzy on the underside.

Numerous cultivars exist and more are released every year, thus a full listing is impossible. While *Buddleja davidii* is the most popular species, *B. globosa* (orange ball bush) from southern Chile is dependable in tropical areas where it is grown for its orange globular flower heads. *Buddleja alternifolia* (fountain butterfly bush), which blooms on old wood, has lilac-colored flowers in spring on cascading branches. Several interspecific hybrids (hybrids between two species) are available. *Buddleja lindleyana,* a suckering shrub which may be overly aggressive, is widely grown.

Culture Butterfly bush prefers well-drained, fertile soil and full sun. Remove winter-killed stems and deadhead spent flowers to encourage continued bloom. Cutting back severely in spring will increase the size and number of flowers as well as promote a denser, more compact form. Plants tend to self-sow, so unwanted seedlings should be removed. Fertilize lightly in spring before growth begins. Root-knot nematodes may attack the roots in some areas, severely limiting the use of this plant. Furthermore, it has demonstrated an invasive tendency in some parts of its range.

Say: kal-ih-KAR-puh a-mer-ih-KAY-na
Salt tolerance: Slight
Size: 6–8 ft. tall/4–8 ft. wide
Origin: United States from Maryland south to Florida and west into Texas

Hardiness: USDA Zones 6–10
Family: Lamiaceae (Mint)
Other name: American beautyberry, French mulberry
Propagation: Seeds; semihardwood cuttings; volunteers

of beautyberries that range in size, hardiness, foliar quality and refinement. A white-fruited form called *Callicarpa americana* var. *lactea* is available. The white berries are especially prominent in the winter landscape after the leaves have fallen. Berries of all the beautyberries are attractive to birds.

The Japanese beautyberry (*Callicarpa japonica*) is hardier and a bit more refined than our native, but it will still reach six to eight feet in height and spread. China's version (*C. bodinieri*) is moderately coarse in texture, about the same size as Japanese beautyberry, and has bluish fruits. It may not be tolerant of the hot, humid climate of the South. More graceful and refined than the others is *C. dichotoma* from China and Japan. Foliage is denser, smaller, and darker colored, and fruit is bright lilac and prolific.

In spring, yellow-green leaves appear, and tiny lilac flowers bloom in clusters from the leaf axils. Flowers are followed by green fruits. Fall brings a startling but delightful change. The fruits change to vibrant violet and are prominently displayed along the length of the stems. The shrub assumes an even looser, more open form as the weight of the berries pulls the stems down.

There are several species

Culture Beautyberry is very adaptable to even the poorest soil. Either full sun or partial shade works well, but foliage is denser and more flowers and fruit are produced in full sun. The drought-tolerant plant requires well-drained soil. Severe pruning can be done in late winter or early spring.

Say: kal-ee-KAN-thus FLOR-id-us
Salt tolerance: Slight to none
Size: 6–10 ft. tall/6–12 ft. wide
Origin: Southeastern United States
Hardiness: USDA Zones 5–9
Family: Calycanthaceae (Sweetshrub)

Other names: Carolina allspice, strawberry shrub, pineapple shrub
Propagation: Seeds; cuttings; layers; removal of suckers

seed pod

Sweetshrub is a deciduous shrub that is highly prized for its fragrant blossoms. From April through July, the two-inch-wide, reddish-brown flowers with straplike petals perfume their area with a fragrance that has been described as a mixture of pineapple, strawberry, and banana. Interesting, urn-shaped fruits follow the blooms and sometimes persist throughout the winter.

No serious insect or disease problems are associated with sweetshrub. Its main problem is its suckering habit. Plant it in a natural area or woodland garden where this tendency will not be a problem.

Cultivars of sweetshrub include 'Athens', 'Edith Wilder', and 'Michael Lindsey'. 'Athens' bears greenish-yellow flowers. 'Edith Wilder' has leaves that are more rounded than is typical, and it grows a bit taller than the species. 'Michael Lindsey' has been selected for its attractive, glossy foliage, long blooming period, more compact size, and dependable yellow fall foliage color.

If you are lucky enough to find sweetshrub growing in the wild, do not remove it or tamper with it. In Florida, it is an endangered species that is in imminent danger of extinction in the wild. Do not plant where livestock graze. It contains a substance similar to strychnine that is poisonous if ingested.

Culture Sweetshrub is very undemanding in the landscape. Plant it in almost any well-drained, acid soil in full sun to partial shade. If desired, prune after flowering to control size. Moist soil is preferred, but established plants can withstand periods of drought.

blossom of 'Athens'

Camellia japonica, C. sasanqua
Camellia

Say: kuh-MEE-lee-uh juh-PON-ih-kuh;
   C. suh-SAN-kwuh
Salt tolerance: Slight
Size: 6–12+ ft. tall/6–12+ ft. wide
Origin: China, Japan
Hardiness: USDA Zones 7–9

Family: Theaceae (Tea)
Other names: Sasanqua, japonica
Propagation: Grafting; layering;
   seeds (may not come true to
   type); cuttings

Camellias are prized for their showy flowers and evergreen, glossy foliage. With appropriate selections, gardeners can have camellias in flower for five or six months.

More than 2,300 cultivars of named camellias are recognized by the American Camellia Society. Embellishing our landscapes are cultivars of Japanese camellia (*Camellia japonica*), sasanqua camellia (*C. sasanqua*), tea-oil

camellia (*C. oleifera*), and other species (*C. sinensis, C. reticulata* and *C. salvenensis*).

Culture Camellias should be planted in partial shade. Acid, well-drained soil that is rich in organic matter is preferred. Maintain a two- to four-inch layer of organic mulch around the base of camellias, but keep it a few inches away from the stem.

The American Camellia Society recommends applying fertilizer in early spring, after the blooming season and danger of freezing weather has passed. It advises an application of 16-4-8 slow-release fertilizer with trace elements at the rate of one tablespoon per foot of height. About four months after the first feeding, apply 5-10-15 with trace elements. In October, a small feeding of 0-20-10 should aid in bloom production. Young plants should be fertilized regularly; however, older, established plants may not require fertilizer at all.

Tea scale and spider mites are the most frequently encountered camellia pests. Diseases include die back, petal blight, occasional root rot, and algal leaf spot. Effective control can be achieved with a variety of insecticides or fungicides. Cultural practices, such as providing air space in and around shrubs and removing spent blossoms, help to prevent diseases.

Cephalanthus occidentalis
Buttonbush

Say: sef-uh-LAN-thus ok-sih-den-TAY-liss

Salt tolerance: Slight

Size: 6–12 ft. tall/4–12 ft. wide

Origin: Eastern half of North America; Texas, New Mexico, Arizona, and California

Hardiness: USDA Zones 4–10

Family: Rubiaceae (Madder)

Other names: Button bush, honey-bells, button-willow, honey balls

Propagation: Softwood or hardwood cuttings; seeds

in woodland areas, edges of ponds, native plant gardens, water retention areas, or any damp place. Several varieties have been identified.

Buttonbush is a multistemmed, deciduous plant that normally has a loose, open form. Tiny, tubular flowers with projecting styles that give it a pincushion-like appearance are borne on ball-shaped heads about one inch in diameter. Creamy white flowers bloom in summer and are moderately ornamental and somewhat fragrant. Flower heads give way to hard, spherical fruits that are green and then turn brown. Medium to dark green leaves are late to leaf out in spring. Branches are usually green when young but turn brown at maturity.

Spherical, honey-scented flowers are attractive to bees, butterflies, and hummingbirds. Although fast-growing and short-lived, buttonbush forms impenetrable thickets that provide valuable cover and food for wildlife, especially shorebirds and waterfowl.

Use buttonbush for naturalizing

Culture Buttonbush is a wet-area plant that likes full sun to light shade. It is easily grown in wet soil, including flooded areas and shallow, standing water. It also adapts to a wide range of soils, except dry ones. No pests or diseases are of concern, but the plant can be short-lived. Rejuvenation pruning can keep it from becoming sprawling and ungainly. Plants can be cut back nearly to the ground to revitalize.

Chaenomeles speciosa
Flowering Quince

Say: kee-no-MAY-leez spee-see-OH-suh
Salt tolerance: Slight to moderate
Size: 6–10 ft. tall/6–10 ft. wide
Origin: China
Hardiness: USDA Zones 4–9

Family: Rosaceae (Rose)
Other name: Japanese quince
Propagation: Cuttings (softwood, semihardwood, or hardwood); layering; seeds; suckers

Flowering quince is a deciduous shrub with a tangled mass of spiny branches. The outline is quite variable and may be erect or rambling. Waxy one and one-half-inch flowers that emerge anywhere from January to March in the South are showy in a mostly dormant landscape. Single or double flowers may be red, salmon, pink, or white.

Fruit is an astringent, hard, yellow, two-inch applelike pome that can be made into a tasty jelly.

Use flowering quince as a hedge or barrier plant or in a shrub border. Tall types can be used as specimens or can be espaliered to accent a wall or fence.

Three distinct species of flowering quince are *Chaenomeles speciosa, C. japonica,* and *C. ×superba* (a cross between the two). Many cultivars exist. Some of the most common include 'Cameo' (double apricot-pink flowers), 'Jet Trail' (white), 'Minerva' (cherry red), 'Nivalis' (white), 'Spitfire' (vivid red), 'Texas Scarlet' (red), and 'Toyo-Nishiki' (pink, white, red, and combination-colored flowers on the same branch).

Culture Flowering quince is an adaptable, easy-to-grow shrub that does best in full sun. It is tolerant of dry soil, but will develop chlorosis in high-pH soil. Periodic pruning improves bloom. Old canes and suckers can be removed every year, or shrubs can be completely rejuvenated by pruning all limbs six to twelve inches above the soil immediately after flowering.

Problems include its susceptibility to apple scab and fireblight. Scale, mites, and aphids can also be troublesome. Because of its twigginess and thorns, leaves and debris can collect in the plant and cause it to be unsightly.

Clethra alnifolia
Sweet Pepperbush

Say: KLETH-ra al-nee-FOH-lee-uh
Salt tolerance: High
Size: 3–10 ft. tall/2–5 ft. wide
Origin: Eastern United States and west to Texas
Hardiness: USDA Zones 4–9

Family: Clethraceae (Sweet Pepperbush)
Other name: Summersweet
Propagation: Division of clumps or rooted cuttings (cultivars); seeds (the species)

Park Seed

Clethra 'Rosea'

Ted Bodner

Culture Clethra performs best in partial shade in moist to wet, acid, fertile, organic soil. It adapts to a wide range of conditions, including sun and occasionally dry soil. Heavy pruning will remove dead wood, promote compactness, or rejuvenate. Since it flowers on new growth of the current season, pruning can be done in late winter before new growth begins. While pests and diseases are not usually a problem, mites can proliferate if the soil becomes too dry. High salt tolerance makes it an excellent choice for seaside gardens.

White or shell pink to light pink flowers emerge in summer and last for two to three weeks. They are fragrant, about four inches long, and about three-fourths of an inch wide. The fluffy, bottlebrush-like flowers are born in three- to six-inch spikes and attract many butterflies, bees, and hummingbirds. Leaves are medium to dark green, turning clear yellow in fall. Fruiting stalks have many miniature, oval capsules with elongated styles. Although noticeable and persistent throughout the winter, they are not particularly ornamental.

Clethra often suckers with age to form tight colonies. This can be an asset for naturalized situations but might prove a liability in highly maintained landscapes. It is rare to find among the flowering shrubs one that blooms well in shade, so this is a great addition to shady spots where color is needed.

Popular cultivars include 'Hummingbird', a compact and spreading form that tops out at about three feet tall and wide. Other popular cultivars are 'Anne Bidwell', 'Cottondale', 'Ruby Spice', and 'Rosea'.

Deutzia gracilis
Slender Deutzia

Say: DOOT-zee-uh GRASS-il-is
Salt tolerance: Moderate to slight
Size: 2–5 ft. tall/2–5 ft. wide
Origin: Japan

Hardiness: USDA Zones 4–8
Family: Hydrangeaceae (Hydrangea)
Other name: Deutzia
Propagation: Softwood cuttings

Richard Webb

Proven Winners

capsules that are ornamentally insignificant.

Deutzia is a free-flowering shrub that ushers in the spring season and then fades into the background for the rest of the year. There are several species in the genus and several hybrids that are garden worthy. Two popular cultivars of *D. gracilis* are 'Nikko', which at two feet tall and four feet wide can be used as a groundcover or dense low mound, and 'Variegata', which has leaves that are broadly margined with white. Chardonnay Pearls® 'Duncan' retains yellow foliage after the flowers have finished.

Slender deutzia is a small, fine-textured deciduous shrub with a mounded form. Pure white, half-inch-diameter flowers bloom in mid spring for one to two weeks. Cup-shaped flowers are borne in long clusters along the stem, and during its bloom time, the plant is literally covered with flowers. Simple leaves about one to three inches long and one-half an inch wide are arranged opposite each other along the stem. Leaves are medium green in color and have unequal serrations along the margins. Fruits are dry, brown

Culture Slender deutzia prefers full sun to partial shade and moist, well-drained, fertile soil. However, it is adaptable to relatively poor soil, variable soil pH, and occasional drought. No insects or diseases are of major concern. Prune immediately after flowering to remove winter-killed stems. Plants can be cut back to the ground every three or four years for total rejuvenation. Such drastic pruning can improve the looks of plants that appear unkempt. Because of a shallow root system, plants are easily transplanted.

Erythrina herbacea
Cherokee Bean

Say: er-ith-RY-nuh hur-BAY-see-uh
Salt tolerance: High
Size: 5–10 ft. tall/8–12 ft. wide
Origin: Southeastern United States and Mexico
Hardiness: USDA Zones 8–11

Family: Fabaceae (Bean)
Other names: Cardinal spear, coral bean
Propagation: Seeds sown on top of the ground, uncovered; cuttings

E. crista-galli
(coral tree)

E. herbacea
(Cherokee bean)

on the undersides of the leaflets. The stems are also armed with short, recurved spines.

A native legume, coral bean provides a splash of red in spring just in time for the hummingbirds and again in autumn, when the beans burst open to reveal bright red seeds that are attractive but poisonous. Although evergreen in the tropics, it gets killed to the ground each year in places where freezing weather occurs, which limits its height.

Related to the coral bean is the coral tree (*Erythrina crista-galli*). This shrub or small tree is sometimes called the crybaby tree or Christ's tears because nectar drips from the blossoms like teardrops. Dark crimson and scarlet flowers bloom in several waves between spring and fall. It is hardy in USDA Zones 8B to 10, and likes full sun and well-drained but moist soil.

Culture Cherokee bean grows well in full sun to partial shade. It likes damp, well-drained acid to slightly alkaline soil, and is drought tolerant once established. Few pests are of concern, but appearance will be improved if dead stems are cut back to the ground before new growth begins in spring.

Bright red tubular flowers are borne on narrow, leafless spikes and contrast sharply with the plant's green foliage. The compound leaves are composed of three shallow-lobed leaflets six to eight inches long that have prickles on their midribs and

Say: yoo-ON-ih-mus a-mer-ih-KAH-nus

Salt tolerance: None

Size: 4–8 ft. tall/4–8 ft. wide

Origin: Eastern North America, and west to Oklahoma and east Texas

Hardiness: USDA Zones 5–9

Family: Celastraceae (Bittersweet)

Other names: American strawberry-bush, hearts-a-burstin', bursting heart

Propagation: Greenwood cuttings taken in summer; seeds after three months of cold treatment; division of root clumps in winter

opened seedpod

Culture Strawberry bush prefers humus-rich, well-drained but moist, slightly acid soil, and partial to full shade. Water and mulch well in hot, dry environments. The plant will withstand heavy pruning. Susceptibility to Euonymus scale and crown gall may limit its use in the landscape.

Strawberry bush occurs naturally in the woods underneath the shade of taller trees. Locate it where its interesting fruits can be appreciated, for the bursting fruit is quite attractive. Expect the bush to spread a bit, forming loose, open clumps.

Inconspicuous, greenish-purple flowers give way to warty scarlet capsules that open in fall to reveal bright scarlet seeds. The fruit show lasts for about a month, and then the leaves provide fall color by turning shades of orange and red. Strawberry bush is a loose, suckering, green-stemmed deciduous shrub.

Place strawberry bush in a native, mixed border or mass it in a woodland setting. It is a good addition to a wildlife habitat. Bees, butterflies, and hummingbirds visit the flowers, and seeds are eaten by many birds and small mammals. Deer browse the foliage. Although the fruits have several medicinal purposes, they are poisonous and should not be consumed.

Fatsia

Say: FAT-see-uh juh-PON-ih-kuh
Salt tolerance: Moderate
Size: 6–10 ft. tall/6–10 ft. wide
Origin: Japan

Hardiness: USDA Zones 8–10
Family: Araliaceae (Ginseng)
Other name: Japanese aralia
Propagation: Cuttings; seeds

flowers mature, clusters of round, berrylike fruits about one-eighth of an inch in diameter are produced, which are green at first and then turn black.

Several cultivars are available. 'Moseri' is more compact than the species. 'Aurea' has golden variegated leaves, and 'Variegata' has white variegation patterns dispersed over the leaf. 'Spider Web' has dark green leaves with speckled variegation. Additional cultivars can be found that have variously variegated or patterned leaves.

Bold, glossy, deeply lobed, evergreen leaves eight to ten inches across and just a bit shorter in length lend a tropical look to the landscape. Creamy white flowers bloom in winter. Since many of the one-inch, circular flower clusters are produced on stems held well above the foliage, they are visually significant. As the

Culture If fatsia is to do its best, it should be planted in loose, well-drained but moist, slightly acid soil. Partial or full shade, especially in the afternoon, is necessary. Even winter sun and wind can cause injury. Improve the looks of overgrown plants by cutting the longest stems off at ground level. Fatsia is generally trouble free, but scale insects and mealy bugs may sometimes be bothersome.

Although Japanese aralia is a great landscape plant, it is also ideal as a container plant on a shaded deck or patio. A good performance can be expected when it is grown as an indoor houseplant, though care must be taken to provide it with bright light but no direct sun.

Forsythia ×intermedia

Forsythia

Say: for-SITH-ee-a × in-ter-MEE-dee-uh
Salt tolerance: Moderate
Size: 8–10 ft. tall/10–12 ft. wide
Origin: China, Korea
Hardiness: USDA Zones 5–8

Family: Oleaceae (Olive)
Other name: Border forsythia
Propagation: Seeds (germination improved after stratification); easy by hardwood cuttings

Forsythia rarely escapes into natural areas, but it will persist around old homesites and turn wild when the site is abandoned or the house removed. Performance seems to be best in the middle part of the U.S. Those in the Deep South never seem to achieve the prominence in the landscape of specimens growing farther north. In the extreme northern areas of its hardiness, the blooms are often killed by freezing weather.

Forsythia ×intermedia is a hybrid of *F. suspensa* (weeping forsythia) and *F. viridissima* (greenstem forsythia). Bright yellow flowers emerge before the foliage and last for two or three weeks in spring. Both upright and arching shoots grow on the plant, which gives it a distinctive form. Fall color may sometimes be significant, with leaves turning deep burgundy. Forsythia fruits are inconspicuous dry capsules.

When forsythia is not in bloom it is nondescript. It can be a rampant grower that is difficult to keep looking neat in the landscape. Other species of *Forsythia* exist, as well as some interspecific hybrids and many cultivars, all of which were bred for different characteristics.

Culture Forsythia needs full sun for best flowering, but will also tolerate dappled shade. Almost any soil will do, and once established it grows well in urban conditions and tolerates considerable drought. Although tolerant of heavy pruning and shearing, too much will destroy its natural form. Plants should be pruned immediately after spring flowering by thinning out crowded stems from the center. Cutting back to the ground will revitalize old plants.

Gardenia jasminoides

Gardenia

Say: gar-DEEN-ee-uh jaz-min-OY-deez
Salt tolerance: Slight
Size: 4–6 ft. tall/4–6 ft. wide
Origin: China, Taiwan, Japan
Hardiness: USDA Zones 7B–10

Family: Rubiaceae (Madder)
Other name: Cape jasmine
Propagation: Cuttings of semihardwood stems; layering; seeds

'Radicans' or 'Prostrata', or the variegated *G. jasminoides* 'Radicans Variegata' for a low-growing groundcover, or choose larger cultivars where plants of greater size are needed.

'Radicans Variegata'

Few plants offer flowers as fragrant as those of gardenia. Lustrous, dark green leaves make a good background for the creamy white flowers. Large forms of the evergreen shrub provide an excellent backdrop for beds and borders, while low-growing prostrate cultivars are used as groundcovers or small-scale shrubs. Fruit is a small, relatively inconspicuous berry.

Gardenia, named by Linnaeus in honor of botanist Alexander Garden, is a genus of about 250 species. *Gardenia jasminoides* has been called by several names (synonyms), including *G. augusta, G. grandiflora, G. schlechteri,* and *G. florida.*

'Mystery'

Many cultivars of *Gardenia jasminoides* are in existence, and they vary in flower size and form, blooming time and duration, and shrub habit and size. Choose *G. jasminoides*

Culture Gardenia prefers sun to partial shade and acid, moist, well-drained soil that is high in organic matter. Apply a complete, slow-release fertilizer in early spring and again in early fall. Protect from extreme winter temperatures, and do any pruning that is needed immediately after flowering.

Gardenia is susceptible to a host of insect pests such as aphids, spider mites, thrips, white flies, and scale insects. Control them by using insecticidal soap or horticultural oil. Gardenia is susceptible to nematode damage, so varieties grafted onto nematode-resistant rootstock are preferred. Gardeners in Zones 9 and 10 can select plants grafted onto the rootstock of *Gardenia thunbergia,* which is nematode resistant.

Hibiscus syriacus
Althea

Say: high-BISS-kuss seer-ee-AY-kuss
Salt tolerance: Moderate
Size: 8–12 ft. tall/4–10 ft. wide
Origin: China and India
Hardiness: USDA Zones 5–9

Family: Malvaceae (Mallow)
Other names: Althaea (spelling variant), rose of Sharon, shrub althea
Propagation: Seeds; cuttings

lavender with red throat

'Blue Bird'

Wayside Gardens

throat 'Helene', the beautiful pink 'Aphrodite', lavender 'Minerva', and more recently, the lavender-blue 'Bluebird'.

Rose of Sharon grows into a large shrub or small, multitrunked tree that blooms in summer. Five-petaled, two- to four-inch flowers produced on the current season's growth may be white, pink, magenta, violet, blue, or combinations of these. Flowers may be single, double, or semidouble, and some have a dark-colored splotch in the center. Deciduous, three-lobed, coarsely toothed, two- to four-inch, medium to dark green leaves are late to leaf out in spring.

Some altheas were introduced by the National Arboretum during the '60s and '70s that are sterile triploids. They have larger flowers that bloom earlier than the species, and they set no seeds. Cultivars include the pure white 'Diana', the white with maroon

Culture Althea prefers well-drained, acid soil and full sun, but some shade is tolerated. Water newly planted shrubs every few days until they become established, and then water as needed to maintain slightly moist soil. Prune lightly in spring to promote larger flowers if desired.

Usually althea is easy to grow and requires little care. However, bud drop can occur if plants receive too much or too little water. A layer of mulch will help keep moisture levels constant. Too much fertilizer can also cause buds to drop and increase aphid infestations. Althea is susceptible to breakage at the crotch because of poor collar formation, and the wood is generally weak and breaks easily.

Hydrangea macrophylla
Bigleaf Hydrangea

Say: hy-DRAN-jee-uh (or hy-DRAIN-juh) mak-roh-FIL-uh
Salt tolerance: Moderate
Size: 3–6 ft. tall/3–6 ft. wide +
Origin: Japan and Korea

Hardiness: USDA Zones 6–9
Family: Hydrangeaceae (Hydrangea)
Other names: French, mophead, or lacecap hydrangea; hortensia
Propagation: Cuttings; layering

'Penny Mac', 'Blushing Bride', 'Mini Penny', and others.

Bigleaf hydrangeas steal the show in late spring and summer with their attractive, large green leaves and showy flower clusters. The cultivars are divided into two different groups. Hortensias, informally called mopheads, have large, showy clusters of sterile blooms. Lacecaps have flat heads with tiny fertile flowers in the center surrounded by larger-petaled, sterile flowers.

In most cultivars, of which there are many, the flower color varies according to the acidity of the soil. Flowers are blue in acid soil and pink in alkaline soil. In neutral soil the flowers are purple or lavender. White-flowered varieties do not change color with variations in soil pH.

Remontant (reblooming) types have the ability to flower almost all summer since they produce new flower buds throughout the summer. These that flower on new wood have extended the flowering time, and many new ones are entering the market. Look for such rebloomers as Endless Summer™ 'Bailmer', 'David Ramsey', 'Decatur Blue', 'Oak Hill',

Culture Provide dappled sun in the morning and protection from hot afternoon sun. Well-drained, moist soil that is rich in organic matter is best. Mulch is beneficial in summer to conserve moisture and in winter to protect canes from severe freezes. The north or east side of a building with cool, moist soil is normally a good environment.

Pests are few, and usually no spraying or other measures are necessary to maintain good health. Pruning should be done immediately after flowering. Some old canes should be removed along with any dead branches. New shoots should not be pruned because they will bear next year's flowers. This rule does not apply to the remontant (reblooming) types.

Hydrangea paniculata
Peegee Hydrangea

Say: hy-DRAN-jee-uh (or hy-DRAIN-juh) pan-ick-yoo-LAY-tuh
Salt tolerance: Unknown
Size: 8–20 ft. tall/8–20 ft. wide
Origin: Japan, China

Hardiness: USDA Zones 3–8
Family: Hydrangeaceae (Hydrangea)
Other names: Panicle hydrangea, tree hydrangea
Propagation: Softwood cuttings

'Limelight'

'Grandiflora' is not recommended for the Deep South, some other cultivars have been grown successfully. Some to try are 'Limelight', 'Tardiva', 'Pinky Winky', 'Quick Fire', 'Chantilly Lace', and others.

'Pinky Winky'

Peegees are large, coarse-textured, deciduous shrubs to small trees that bloom in summer with large, showy panicles (clusters) of white flowers. Blossoms exhibit a combination of showy sterile flowers and fertile flowers. The name "paniculata" comes from the fact that the flowers are panicle-shaped (like a cone), and not rounded or flat-topped. Although flowers start out white or pistachio green, many of them turn shades of pink as they mature.

Peegee is the best known *Hydrangea paniculata.* This nickname comes from its botanical name, *Hydrangea paniculata* 'Grandiflora' (PG). Many nurserymen use the nickname "peegee" to refer to all of the paniculatas, although in fact it originally referred only to 'Grandiflora'. Following the lead of these nurserymen, I have chosen to use the term "peegee" to refer to all of the paniculata hydrangeas.

While *Hydrangea paniculata*

Culture Panicle hydrangeas appreciate moist but well-drained, fertile, organic soil. Several hours of sun are needed for best performance, although in the Deep South a little protection from the hot afternoon sun is beneficial. Prune at any time except immediately before flowering. Plants can be trained into small trees by selectively pruning lower branches. Flower color is not influenced by the pH of the soil.

Hydrangea quercifolia
Oakleaf Hydrangea

Say: hy-DRAN-jee-uh (or hy-DRAIN-juh) kwur-sif-FOLE-ee-uh
Salt tolerance: None
Size: 6–10 ft. tall/6–8 ft. wide
Origin: Southeastern United States
Hardiness: USDA Zones 5–9

Family: Hydrangeaceae (Hydrangea)
Other names: None
Propagation: Seeds; layering; division; cuttings; removal of suckers

The oakleaf hydrangea is a deciduous shrub bearing handsome, five-lobed leaves reminiscent of the red oak. Young leaves are yellowish-green on top and fuzzy and whitish underneath. Leaves are arranged in pairs opposite each other and are four to twelve inches long and about as wide. In summer they darken to deep green, and in fall they turn bronze or crimson colors.

Elongated clusters of fertile and sterile white flowers bloom in early summer. Individual flower spikes are borne in erect clusters four to twelve inches long that taper to a point. Flowers turn pinkish-purple and then brown as they age. Plants can be attractive in winter, when the older stems exfoliate to reveal cinnamon-colored inner bark.

Several cultivars are available, including 'Harmony', 'PeeWee', 'Snowflake', and 'Snow Queen'. Oakleaf hydrangea grows quite large, so make sure to allow room for it to grow. The shrub makes an excellent specimen, and it looks good at the edge of woods or in a naturalized area. Use oakleaf hydrangea in the landscape to provide a focal point or flowering accent, or place it in a mixed shrub border.

Culture Optimal growing conditions include moist, fertile, well-drained soil and full sun to partial shade. Even though oakleaf hydrangea is quite drought tolerant, it flourishes in mulched areas with a cool, moist root environment. The species seems quite disease and insect resistant. If pruning is necessary, it should be done immediately after flowering. Remove basal suckers as they form, unless a colony of plants is wanted.

Illicium floridanum
Florida Anise

Say: il-LISS-ee-um flor-ih-DAY-num
Salt tolerance: Slight
Size: 10–15 ft. tall/6–10 ft. wide
Origin: Florida Panhandle to
    southeastern Louisiana

Hardiness: USDA Zones 7–10
Family: Illiciaceae (Illicium)
Other names: Purple anise,
    stinkbush, star anise
Propagation: Cuttings; seeds

'Shady Lady'

Culture Florida anise is at home in shade to partial shade and appreciates well-drained, moist, acid soil. Pruning once a year before growth begins in spring will help to maintain a shrub form, or it can be trained into a small tree by removing some of the lower branches. Very few pests attack this native plant.

green seed pod

blossom

Florida anise is a broad-leaved evergreen shrub or small tree with leathery but glossy leaves two to six inches long and about an inch or two wide. Two-inch starlike flowers with many slender maroon petals are somewhat malodorous. The leaves, however, smell of anise when they are crushed or torn. Flowers are followed by seeds held in inconspicuous star-shaped papery follicles, which explode when ripe.

Several cultivars are available. 'Album', 'Semmes', and 'Alba' have white flowers; 'Halley's Comet' has an extended bloom time and darker flowers; and 'Shady Lady' has variegated leaves and pink flowers. Never remove Florida anise from the wild, as it is listed as a threatened species in Florida.

Illicium verum (star-anise) from China and Vietnam is the source of a culinary spice and also has several medicinal uses. *Illicium parviflorum* (yellow anise), another Florida native, is useful in the landscape where a hedge is needed. Size is larger (15–20 ft. tall/10–15 ft. wide) than Florida anise, and it can tolerate more sun. It is listed as endangered by the state of Florida. Both Florida natives are toxic and should not be ingested, but they are both useful in landscapes where a large, evergreen shrub or hedge is needed.

Itea virginica
Virginia Sweetspire

Say: eye-TEE-uh vir-JIN-ih-kuh
Salt tolerance: Slight to none
Size: 3–6 ft. tall/5–10 ft. wide
Origin: Southern United States and as far north as New Jersey

Hardiness: USDA Zones 5–9
Family: Grossulariaceae (Currant)
Other names: Itea, Virginia willow
Propagation: Seeds; cuttings; separation of root suckers

'Little Henry'

Proven Winners

Chris Evans

Several cultivars have been selected. 'Henry's Garnet' bears white flowers in clusters six inches long, and the foliage turns rich red-purple in fall. 'Long Spire' is noted for its eight-inch-long flower clusters, and 'Sarah Eve' has pinkish flowers but rather poor fall color. 'Saturnalia' is smaller than the species, and 'Sprich' (Little Henry™) is a compact, mounded plant with smaller clusters of flowers.

Itea is a versatile shrub for the shrub border or woodland garden. Use its suckering habit to advantage by placing it in low spots on the edges of streams or ponds to check erosion. Flowers attract butterflies, and seeds are eaten by birds.

Itea is a deciduous to semievergreen, multistemmed shrub with erect stems that branch only near the top. In early summer, lightly fragrant, showy white flowers are borne in long clusters (racemes) that look somewhat like small bottlebrushes. In fall the deep green leaves change to brilliant red, orange, crimson, and maroon and hold until December or later. Fruiting stalks containing many small capsules persist throughout the winter.

Culture Itea prefers full sun to partial shade in fertile, moist soil, but is adaptable to almost any site, including wet or dry and acid to alkaline soil. Flowers are borne on the previous season's growth, so pruning, if needed, should be done immediately after the flowers fade. Avoid high fertilization since it can lead to aggressiveness in this normally suckering shrub, which spreads by runners and can become invasive in rich soil. No insects or diseases are problematic.

Kalmia latifolia
Mountain Laurel

Say: KAL-mee-uh lat-ih-FOH-lee-uh
Salt tolerance: None
Size: 5–15+ ft. tall/5–12 ft. wide
Origin: Eastern North America
Hardiness: USDA Zones 4A–8

Family: Ericaceae (Heath)
Other name: Calico bush
Propagation: Seeds; cuttings
(difficult); tissue culture of most
cultivars

Dow Gardens

special concern; and in New York they are exploitably vulnerable. Both Connecticut and Pennsylvania claim it as their state flower. The leaves, buds, flowers, and fruits of mountain laurel are poisonous and potentially lethal to humans and livestock. However, white-tailed deer, black bear, and other wildlife use it as winter forage.

Mountain laurel is a rounded, broadleaf evergreen shrub that becomes more open and loose with age. The trunk is contorted and cinnamon colored. In sun the form is dense, but in shade it becomes more sprawling. In late spring, showy, star-shaped flowers bloom in six-inch-diameter clusters (corymbs) at branch tips. Blossoms on the species are normally pink before fading to nearly white. Fruit is a small brown capsule that explodes when dry.

Many cultivars are available. Flower colors range from white to all shades of pink and red. Sometimes buds are intensely colored and flowers open a lighter color. Sizes range from dwarf to tree stature. Thanks to the work of Richard Jaynes, a Connecticut plant breeder, dozens of new cultivars have been introduced. His book, *Kalmia: Mountain Laurel and Related Species*, has much information about these plants.

Never remove plants from native stands. In Florida they are threatened; in Maine they are of

Culture Mountain laurel grows naturally at the edge of woods or where light filters through the forest canopy. It is tolerant of partial shade to full sun and appreciates cool, moist, acid, organic soil. Plant these fibrous-rooted shrubs high and mulch well. Avoid windswept sites to prevent foliar burn. To avoid trouble with leaf spot diseases, choose resistant cultivars and avoid planting in heavy shade. Watch for whitefly, scale, lace bug, and stem borer, and treat if necessary. Apply small amounts of acid-forming fertilizer in spring.

Kerria japonica
Japanese Rose

Say: KER-ee-a juh-PON-ih-kuh
Salt tolerance: None
Size: 3–6 ft. tall/6–9 ft. wide
Origin: Japan and China
Hardiness: USDA Zones 4–9

Family: Rosaceae (Rose)
Other names: Kerria, Japanese kerria,
   Easter rose
Propagation: Cuttings; division

Phillip Oliver

leaves edged in yellow. One cultivar,
'Aureo-vittata', has branches that are
striped green and yellow, but they
often revert to solid green.

Kerria is a deciduous shrub with
many fine, slender stems. Glossy,
smooth, and upright, the arching
stems form a low mass of dense,
twiggy growth. Plants sucker freely
and can colonize an area. The bright
green to yellow-green, zigzagging
stems add color during the winter
when bare of leaves. In spring and
sporadically afterwards, showy
bright yellow flowers bloom. Flowers
are about one and one-half inches
in diameter, and are reminiscent of
an old-fashioned rose with its five
petals. Bright green leaves with
serrated edges are also attractive.

Several cultivars are available.
A double-flowered form named
'Pleniflora' is very popular. Others
with single five-petaled flowers such
as 'Albaflora' and 'Golden Guinea' are
also attractive. Several variegated
types are available, including 'Picta',
which sports creamy white leaf
margins, and 'Aureo-variegata', with

Culture Kerria performs best in
partial to full shade. Although
it grows well in the sun, the
flowers will fade and not be as
showy. Plants are easy to grow
in well-drained, moist, loamy
soil. Irrigate during periods
of drought. Fertilize sparingly
because too much fertilizer will
promote vegetative growth at
the expense of flowers. Remove
dead shoots as needed, and cut
plants back to the ground to
rejuvenate. Prune immediately
after flowering. Some leaf and
twig blight, canker, leaf spot, and
other diseases may cause a few
problems, but usually they are
not serious.

Say: kol-KWIT-zee-uh a-MAH-bih-liss
Salt tolerance: None
Size: 6–10 ft. tall/6–8 ft. wide
Origin: China
Hardiness: USDA Zones 4–8

Family: Linnaeaceae (Twinflower)
Other names: None
Propagation: Seeds; softwood or
    hardwood cuttings

Phillip Oliver

Rob Broekhuis

Although seeds of beautybush germinate readily, they are likely to result in inferior plants with washed-out flower colors. Softwood cuttings root readily and guarantee a plant exactly like the parent.

As plants age, they become leggy, with most of the foliage concentrated at the top. Although beautiful in bloom, the plant is nondescript for the rest of the year. The cultivar 'Pink Cloud' is commonly available, and it has an abundance of bright pink blooms that are larger than the species. 'Rosea' is rarely seen in the trade, but it bears reddish flowers. Dream Catcher™ ('Maradco') has leaves that emerge in bright copper tones and change to yellow, then lime green, and finally to shades of orange and gold, giving multiseason interest.

Beautybush is a large, deciduous, multistemmed shrub with an upright-arching and fountainlike form. Pink bell-shaped clusters (corymbs) of one-inch-long flowers with a yellow throat appear in late spring and are followed by fuzzy pinkish seedheads. Fruit is a persistent, bristly, oval capsule that splits in winter to release seeds. Leaves are dull dark green in summer and turn slightly yellow or red in fall. The light brown bark splits vertically and peels and exfoliates with age.

Culture Beautybush appreciates full sun and ordinary, well-drained soil. It is adaptable to a wide range of soil pH, both acid and alkaline, and is tolerant of drought, heat, and humidity. Prune out the oldest stems every year or so, or cut back to the ground to rejuvenate. Pruning should be done immediately after the flowering period.

Lantana camara hybrids and cultivars

Lantana

Say: lan-TAN-a kuh-MAR-uh
Salt tolerance: High
Size: 1–6 ft. tall/1–6 ft. wide
Origin: West Indies
Hardiness: USDA Zones 8–11

Family: Verbenaceae (Verbena)
Other name: Shrub verbena
Propagation: Cuttings of firm young shoots in spring; hardwood cuttings in fall; layering

'Luscious Grape'

'Luscious Tropical Fruit'

'Gold Mound'

Low, spreading cultivars of *Lantana camara* are among the most commonly grown shrubs in the South. Plants are covered with two-inch, disk-shaped flower heads throughout the summer. These flowers are attractive to butterflies, but they are extremely poisonous to humans and can cause death.

Whiteflies, mites, caterpillars, and lantana lace bugs are sometimes problematic and may need to be controlled. Prune during the summer by lightly shearing the tip growth to encourage repeat blooming. If plants become too large for their space, they can be pruned back by up to a third of their height and spread. In winter, dead limbs can be pruned back to ground level to keep the garden looking neat. Growth will resume in spring.

Choose cultivars such as 'Gold Mound', 'New Gold', 'Lucious', and 'Patriot'. These sterile hybrids are usually a cross between trailing lantana (*Lantana montevidensis*) and common lantana (*Lantana camara*). Such hybridization often results in sterility. However, exercise caution, as the so-called sterile cultivars can revert to fertile seed-bearing forms, which may become invasive. The species, *Lantana camara,* is a Category I invasive plant in Florida and is a weed worldwide.

Culture Lantana prefers full sun and well-drained, moderately fertile soil. Even though plants are drought tolerant, they benefit from being watered during periods of dry weather. Avoid overhead watering, which can encourage diseases and root rot. Nutritional needs are low, but a light fertilization in spring is beneficial.

* See page 16.

Lantana montevidensis
Trailing Lantana

Say: lan-TAN-a mon-tay-vid-EN-sis
Salt tolerance: High
Size: 1.5/2 ft. tall/5–6 ft. wide
Origin: South America
Hardiness: USDA Zones 8B–11

Family: Verbenaceae (Verbena)
Other names: Weeping lantana, polecat geranium
Propagation: Cuttings; layering

'White Lightnin''

make the plants more susceptible to diseases. One light application in spring is usually sufficient. *Lantana montevidensis* is more resistant to lantana lace bugs than its cousin, *L. camara.* All species of lantana are poisonous and should be kept out of pastures. Livestock, pets, and children have been poisoned by ingesting berries or foliage of this toxic plant.

Cultivars of trailing lantana can be selected, such as 'Malan's Gold', which sports yellow and green foliage and rose-colored flowers. 'Pot of Gold' has bright yellow flowers. 'White Lightnin'' has pure white flowers, and 'Lavendar Swirl' has white flowers that gradually deepen to pale lavender and finally to a rich lavender.

Weeping, vinelike stems are covered nearly year-round with clusters of verbena-like lavender, white, or yellow flowers that are about one inch in diameter. Small, neat, closely veined leaves may turn red to purple in colder months. Tops will die back at about 20ºF, but plants will recover in the spring.

Pruning can be done to keep trailing lantana within bounds. Stubbing back to the ground occasionally, especially in spring to remove dead branches, is beneficial. Fertilize sparingly, as too much fertilizer may suppress flowering and

Culture Trailing lantana flowers most heavily in full sun. Although tolerant of poor soil and drought, better performance can be expected when watered weekly. Soil should be well drained or root rot may be a problem. Trailing lantana exhibits outstanding heat, wind, and salt tolerance, making it a good choice for people who live near bodies of salt water. Nectar-laden blossoms make it a natural choice for butterfly gardens. Plants are poisonous to livestock and pets.

Doghobble

Say: loo-KOH-thoh-ee ack-sil-LAIR-iss
Salt tolerance: None
Size: 2–6 ft. tall/6–10 ft. wide
Origin: Eastern United States from
    Virginia south

Hardiness: USDA Zones 5B–9
Family: Ericaceae (Heath)
Other name: Coastal leucothoe
Propagation: Seeds; cuttings

Ted Bodner

Richard Carter

Several leaf spot diseases infect leucothoe, and root rot may occur if soil is not well drained. Protect from dry winds and drought.

Mass doghobble in the garden as a groundcover, or use it as an underplanting for larger shrubs to help soften the stiffer shrubs in the landscape. The stoloniferous habit causes it to spread and form colonies. Both leaves and flower nectar are poisonous.

Several cultivars are available. 'Compacta', 'Augusta Evans Wilson', 'Beulah', and 'Macaria' are dwarf selections. 'Dodd's Variegated' has leaves mottled with white, and 'Greensprite' has arching, somewhat stiff branches and reaches a height of six feet. 'Sara's Choice' features profuse blooms and reddish new foliage on a four-foot-tall plant.

Coastal leucothoe is a graceful, informal, evergreen shrub. Glossy, dark green leaves turn purple-bronze in winter, and the green stems tend to zigzag at each leaf tip. Slightly fragrant, small, bell-shaped white to pinkish-white flowers hang in clusters (racemes) from the leaf axils in spring. Fruit is an inconspicuous brown capsule.

Culture For best results, careful attention must be given to the cultural needs of this plant. Full to partial shade is required, and if sun is part of the exposure, it should be morning sun. Although soil should be almost constantly moist, it should also be well drained, highly acid and richly organic. Prune out older center canes after bloom to rejuvenate.

Lindera benzoin
Spicebush

Say: lin-DEER-ruh ben-ZOH-in
Salt tolerance: Moderate
Size: 8–12 ft. tall/ 8–12 ft. wide
Origin: Eastern North America
Hardiness: USDA Zones 4–9

Family: Lauraceae (Laurel)
Other names: Common spicebush, northern spicebush, Benjamin bush
Propagation: Seeds

Culture Spicebush prefers moist, well-drained soil and full sun to partial shade. Best fall color develops in sunny areas, but the shrub tolerates full shade. Plant in masses for best flowering and fruiting. Be sure to include a male or two to pollinate the female flowers.

Small greenish-yellow flowers held close to the branches before the leaves emerge in early spring have led some to call the spicebush "wild forsythia." The flowers on female plants are followed by scarlet, oval fruit about half an inch in diameter that have a peppery taste and scent. Aromatic light green leaves turn golden yellow in fall. The deciduous shrub is rounded with a loose, open form.

Plants are dioecious (male and female flowers on separate plants). Flowers of the male are larger and showier than the female blossoms. Females will not set fruit without a male pollinator in the vicinity.

Spicebush is a wonderful addition to a garden for wildlife. Foliage is used as a larval plant for the spicebush and tiger swallowtail butterflies, and its berries are one of the best sources of energy for fall migrating birds. Flowers are an important source of nectar for butterflies and other pollinating insects.

Dow Gardens

Spicebush is attractive in the landscape for its blooms, attractive fall color, and red berries. Use it in shrub borders, in shade or woodland gardens, or in naturalized areas. Berries can be dried and crushed to be used like allspice or black pepper. They also make delicious jelly, and the leaves can be used to make a fragrant tea.

Say: lor-oh-PET-al-um chi-NEN-see (variety) ROO-brum
Salt tolerance: Slight to none
Size: 4–12 ft. tall/4–12 ft. wide
Origin: China, Japan, and southeastern Asia
Hardiness: USDA Zones 7–10

Family: Hamamelidaceae (witchhazel)
Other names: Chinese witchhazel, fringe flower, Chinese fringe flower
Propagation: Seeds; cuttings; layering of lower limbs

'Blush' foliage

'Ruby'

'Burgundy' has electric, dark pink flowers and rich, reddish-purple foliage that matures to purplish-green. It can reach a height of 14 or more feet. 'Blush' has lighter, pink-tinged leaves and paler, rose-colored flowers, and grows about six feet tall and four to five feet wide. 'Ruby', the baby of the species, matures at four or five feet tall and is an excellent choice for the landscape in places where space does not allow for one of the larger-growing cultivars. Other selections are 'Monraz' and 'Zhuzou'.

Use loropetalum as a single specimen plant, or in corner and understory plantings, screens, or mixed shrub borders. Older specimens may serve as small, multitrunked trees if lower branches are removed.

In spring, masses of fringelike magenta blossoms hang in clusters from the ends of branches. For the rest of the year these evergreen shrubs sport attractive leaves in various shades of burgundy, purple, or pink interspersed with green. Branches are held outward in horizontal layers. Fruit is a woody capsule.

Several cultivars are available.

Culture Plant loropetalum in moist but well-drained organic soil in full sun to light shade. Mulch to conserve moisture, as performance will be poor in dry soil. Use azalea/camellia fertilizer to prevent leaf yellowing and to promote the acid soil in which loropetalum thrives. If necessary, prune in late spring as soon as the flowers fade. Appearance is best if the natural shape of the plant is maintained.

Say: ly-OH-nee-uh loo-sid-uh
Salt tolerance: None
Size: 3–10 ft. tall/3–5 ft. wide
Origin: Southeastern United States and Cuba

Hardiness: USDA Zones 7–9
Family: Ericaceae (Heath)
Other names: Shiny lyonia, pink fetterbush
Propagation: Stem cuttings in spring

Richard Carter

James H. Miller

Culture Fetterbush needs acid soil with lots of humus when grown under cultivation. Extensive, interconnected rhizomes sprout and form dense thickets. If necessary, prune immediately after flowering to avoid cutting off next season's blooms, which are formed during the summer. Shrubs are tolerant of moist to fairly dry soil. Irrigate until well established, and provide partial shade.

Fetterbush is an open, arching, evergreen shrub that grows as an understory plant. It can be found in wet habitats such as wet savannas, bogs, and cypress swamps, or in dry pine flatwoods and other dry, scrubby habitats. In spring it bears a multitude of half-inch-long, bell-shaped flowers. Pale pink to pinkish-white, honey-scented flowers hang from the leaf axils in showy clusters that last for several weeks. Following the flowers are woody, round, five-parted capsules about one-third of an inch in diameter. Leaves are simple, alternate, and leathery.

Leaf spot diseases have been problematic with fetterbush. This disease seriously affects its usefulness in some landscape situations.

Several members of the heath family are very similar. *Lyonia ferruginea* (staggerbush) and *L. fruticosa* (coastal plain staggerbush) are both common understory shrubs. *Agarista populifolia* (pipestem) and *Leucothoe axillaris* (doghobble) can be distinguished by the inside of the stem, which is solid in doghobble and chambered in pipestem. All are closely related and hard to distinguish in the field. All are native shrubs that have potential as ornamental plants in Southern landscapes.

Magnolia figo
Banana Shrub

Say: mag-NO-lee-uh FYE-go
Salt tolerance: Slight
Size: 10–15 ft. tall/6–15 ft. wide
Origin: China

Hardiness: USDA Zones 7B–10
Family: Magnoliaceae (Magnolia)
Other names: None
Propagation: Cuttings

Cultivars include 'Stubbs Purple', with flowers that are more purple than the species, and 'Port Wine', which has a compact habit to about six feet tall and flowers with more maroon than the species.

Plant banana shrub for its upright, oval form, fragrant flowers, and dense mass. Place it near a deck or patio or where its pleasant scent can be enjoyed.

A member of the magnolia family, the banana shrub is aptly named, because its scent is reminiscent of bananas. Compact and densely branched, this slow-growing evergreen shrub bears small, creamy yellow, magnolia-like flowers edged with maroon. The fragile flowers shatter easily.

Other features of the banana shrub are interesting, too. Before the blooms burst open, fuzzy buds line the stems. The female floral organs in the center of the flower are rich green and contrast vividly with the flower. They remain after the petals drop to the ground.

Banana shrub may become infested with scale insects. Control can be achieved by using horticultural oil according to package directions.

Culture Banana shrub prefers acid, fertile, well-drained soil and is moderately drought tolerant once established. It performs well in sun or light shade. Establish a strong root system during the first growing season by watering regularly. Sprinkle a general-purpose fertilizer on top of the soil out to the drip line before new growth begins in spring. If a formal appearance is wanted, shear it annually after flowering. If desired, the shrub can be trained into a small, multitrunked tree by limbing up the branches.

Nerium oleander
Oleander

Say: NER-ee-um oh-lee-AN-der
Salt tolerance: High
Size: 4–18 ft. tall/4–18 ft. wide
Origin: Northern Africa, the eastern
Mediterranean basin, and
southeast Asia

Hardiness: USDA Zones 8–10
Family: Apocynaceae (Dogbane)
Other names: None
Propagation: Cuttings

Oleander is an easy-care, evergreen shrub or small tree with long, dark green leaves. During the summer, an abundance of single or double flowers in yellow, white, pink, or red bloom in terminal clusters. It grows well at the seashore, in highway medians with no irrigation, and in other difficult situations.

Prune if necessary to control size or shape. Remove suckers from the base of plants, as they will siphon off energy and inhibit flowering. Although oleander grows naturally into a rounded shrub, it can be pruned into a standard, or treelike, form.

The oleander caterpillar is a serious pest that can defoliate a plant. The adult stage of the caterpillar is sometimes called the polka-dot wasp moth. This moth is easy to recognize. Look for a wasplike moth with body and wings that are a beautiful, iridescent blue-green. The body, wings, legs, and antennae are covered with small white dots, and the tip of the abdomen is bright orange. To control, clip off and destroy infested shoots or spray with a product containing Bt (*Bacillus thuringiensis*).

All parts of oleander are poisonous. Chewing one leaf or twig can send a person to the hospital. Even the smoke resulting from burning the branches can be fatal. Many people suffer dermatitis after handling oleander stems or branches.

Culture Oleander grows and flowers best in full sun. Although it is very drought tolerant, growth is faster and more vigorous when moisture is plentiful. Hardiness varies with variety. Standard types are hardy to the low teens while the dwarf varieties are more tender.

Say: os-MAN-thus FRAY-granz
Salt tolerance: Slight
Size: 10–15 ft. tall/8–10 ft. wide
Origin: Asia
Hardiness: USDA Zones 7B–9

Family: Oleaceae (Olive)
Other names: Sweet osmanthus, tea olive, hardy tea olive
Propagation: Medium wood cuttings

Blossoms of the hardy tea olive are visually inconsequential, but their impact can be significant. The strong fragrance can be smelled

from several hundred feet away. Tiny white flowers bloom in clusters along the stems. Leaves are dark, glossy green, arranged oppositely on the stem, and margins may be finely toothed or smooth.

Sweet olive blooms during the cool season. Expect it to bloom in late fall and again in early spring. If winters are mild, it blooms most of the season.

Osmanthus fragrans var. *aurantiacus* is a variety with striking yellowish-orange flowers. It has larger, coarser-textured foliage than the regular sweet olive, and new growth is reddish-bronze.

The South is fortunate to have its own native sweet olive (*Osmanthus americanus*), commonly called devilwood or wild olive. It ranges from southeastern Louisiana eastward to Florida and north to Virginia. Normally it is associated with moist, fertile, acid soil, but it is tolerant of most conditions. Small, cream-colored flowers are not showy, but they are somewhat fragrant. Blooms are present in March and April. Dark blue berries about one-half inch in diameter ripen in September and provide food for birds and small mammals.

Culture Sweet olive does best in fertile, moist, well-drained, slightly acid soil. Sunlight or partial shade suits it well. Sometimes, when old specimens have become too large as shrubs, they may be reclaimed as small evergreen trees by removing the lower branches. A wind-resistant, long-lived shrub with few plant pests, it is often found in old gardens of the South.

Philadelphus coronarius
Sweet Mockorange

Say: fil-uh-DEL-fuss kor-oh-NAR-ee-us
Salt tolerance: Moderate
Size: 10–12 ft. tall/8–10 ft. wide
Origin: Southern Europe
Hardiness: USDA Zones 4–8

Family: Hydrangeaceae (Hydrangea)
Other names: English dogwood, mockorange
Propagation: Seeds or cuttings; removal of suckers

and 'Variegatus', with handsome variegated foliage, extend the choice range. In addition, *P. coronarius* has been used as a parent with other *Philadelphus* species, and many hybrids are available.

Sweet mockorange is an upright, rounded shrub with stiff, ascending branches that often become leggy with age. White, four-petaled, commonly fragrant (but not always) flowers with prominent yellow stamens bloom in spring. Flowers are one to one-and-one-half inches across, and thousands of them on a tree at one time are an impressive sight. Branches exfoliate in strips to reveal light brown bark.

Some gardeners have had disappointing experiences growing mockorange. All agree that it is quite beautiful every spring and that it attracts the shy orchard orioles, which visit it while it is in bloom to sip its nectar. Many specimens, however, have not even a whiff of fragrance and are nondescript during the rest of the year. In addition, it suckers excessively, especially if the roots are cut or injured. Because of the massive root system, removal of the plant is a laborious task.

Cultivars such as 'Aureus', which has yellow foliage, 'Nanus', which tops out at about four feet tall,

Culture *Philadelphus* prefers full sun but tolerates light shade. Its preference is for moist, well-drained soil high in organic matter, but once established it is drought tolerant and wind resistant. Old plants can be rejuvenated after flowering by cutting old wood back to the ground. Pruning branches at any point other than ground level results in a top-heavy, unattractively shaped shrub. Removal of suckers may be required if a colony is not desired.

Pieris japonica
Japanese Pieris

Say: pee-AIR-iss juh-PON-ih-kuh
Salt tolerance: None
Size: 8–12 ft. tall/6–10 ft. wide
Origin: Japan
Hardiness: USDA Zones 5–8

Family: Ericaceae (Heath)
Other names: Pieris, lily-of-the-valley bush, Japanese andromeda
Propagation: Seeds; rooted cuttings

Dow Gardens

cultivars have been named and have varying characteristics, such as more colorful or longer clusters of flowers or more dramatic leaf coloring.

Pieris floribunda (mountain andromeda) is native to the United States. It has an upright and spreading shape and is best in the cooler regions of the South.

Dow Gardens

Pieris is a multistemmed, upright to spreading, broadleaf, evergreen shrub. During fall and winter, prominent drooping panicles of reddish flower buds decorate the shrub, and in late winter or early spring they open to reveal the lightly scented white or pink flowers. Individual flowers are about one-fourth of an inch long and shaped like an inverted urn, but they are borne in showy, branched, pendulous clusters up to six inches long. Evergreen leaves emerge a rich bronze color, change to bright green, and then mature to dark green. Five-valved brown seed capsules persist throughout the year unless removed.

Pieris is a beautiful shrub if its growing conditions are met. Neutral or alkaline soil, poorly drained soil, or too much sun will predispose it to diseases and insects that lead to decline, dieback, or death. Many

Culture Pieris prefers partial shade and moist, rich, well-drained, acid soil. It grows best in locations sheltered from wind. Remove spent flowers immediately after bloom. Diseases that may attack include dieback (phytophthora) and leaf spot. Lace bug infestations can be a serious problem, and mites, nematodes, and scale may need to be treated. If yellowing foliage or stunted growth indicates the need for fertilization, apply an acid-forming fertilizer at the dripline of the plant.

Say: pit-oh-SPOR-um toe-BYE-ruh
Salt tolerance: High
Size: 10–15 ft. tall/15–20+ ft. wide
Origin: China and Japan
Hardiness: USDA Zones 8–10

Family: Pittosporaceae (Pittosporum)
Other names: Japanese pittosporum, Japanese mock orange
Propagation: Cuttings; seeds

Leathery, glossy leaves arranged alternately and in a whorl around the stem of this evergreen shrub make it attractive enough, but the thousands of fragrant flowers that bloom each spring are memorable. Each flower is only about half an inch wide, but they are borne in clusters three to four inches wide. Flowers that start out white and turn to yellow as they age have a delicious orange-blossom scent. The variegated form has grayish-green leaves with cream-colored, irregular margins. Fruit is a green, three-valved, pear-shaped capsule that turns to brown as it matures.

Several cultivars of *Pittosporum tobira* give homeowners a number of choices. 'Variegata' has gray-green leaves edged with white and may not be as hardy as the species. 'Wheeler's Dwarf' is a compact form that grows about three to four feet tall and wide and is smaller in all aspects than the species. It, too, is less hardy than the tall green pittosporum.

Almost every floral designer who lives in the South either grows this shrub or knows someone who does. The whorled leaves can be substituted for flowers in floral designs, and the stems remain turgid long after they are cut. Cut stems are an important part of the cut flower industry.

Culture Pittosporum is very drought tolerant, but it looks best when provided with adequate moisture. However, root rot may occur if soil is too moist. A place in full sun to light shade is acceptable, but plants will be lankier when grown in shade. Salt tolerance makes it a good choice for seaside plantings. Pittosporum prunes well into almost any shape and can be maintained as a shrub or limbed up into a small tree.

Prunus glandulosa
Dwarf Flowering Almond

Say: PROO-nus glan-doo-LOW-suh
Salt tolerance: Unknown
Size: 4–5 ft. tall/3–4 ft. wide
Origin: China
Hardiness: USDA Zones 4–8

Family: Rosaceae (Rose)
Other names: Pink flowering almond, almond cherry
Propagation: Cuttings; division of clumps

blossoms, while 'Alba Plena' has double white flowers. 'Rosea Plena', sometimes called 'Sinensis', bears double pink flowers and is frequently available in the trade.

Culture Plant dwarf flowering almond in full sun to partial shade. It is adaptable to almost any soil as long as it is well drained. Once established, it is moderately drought tolerant. Prune severely immediately after flowering to promote new stems, which will flower better the following spring than old stems will. This plant is susceptible to several diseases and insects.

Dwarf flowering almond is a deciduous, multistemmed shrub. One of the first things to bloom in early spring, its flowers are often seen at the same time as early-blooming forsythia. Flowers may be pink or white and single or double. Red fruits are rarely produced, and possibly not at all on cultivars with double flowers.

Dwarf flowering almond is nondescript in the summer, fall, and winter landscape. Plants can become thin and wiry if not pruned regularly. Part of the reason for the popularity of this shrub may be that it has been around for so long that many of us remember it in the yards of our parents and grandparents.

Prunus is a large genus of trees and shrubs and includes plums, cherries, peaches, apricots, and almonds. While most are grown for their fruits, many are planted for their attractive blossoms.

Several cultivars of *P. glandulosa* have been selected. 'Alba' and 'Lawrence' bear single white

Punica granatum 'Nana'

Dwarf Pomegranate

Say : PU-ni-kuh gran-AH-tum
Salt tolerance: Moderate
Size: 3–4 ft. tall/3–4 ft. wide
Origin: Iran to the Himalayas in
  northern India

Hardiness: USDA Zones 7–10
Family: Lythraceae (Loosestrife)
Other names: None
Propagation: Cuttings; layering;
  seeds (will not be true to type)

blossoms; 'Pleniflora' and 'Rubra Plena' with double red flowers; and 'Variegata', which has a double, scarlet flower that is streaked with yellowish-white.

If you wish to grow a full-sized pomegranate for its fruit, look for the vigorous and productive 'Wonderful', which originated in Florida. The large, dark purple-red fruit has deep red, juicy pulp.

New bronzy-tinted leaves, which emerge in spring, gradually change to bright green. In May, bright reddish-orange blooms appear. Fruit that follows is two to three inches long and looks like a miniature version of the regular pomegranate. In fall, leaves turn yellow before they shed. Fruits are long lasting and may persist on the tree through the winter.

'Nana', the dwarf form of pomegranate, has more vigor than its large kin. Since it is self fertile, it needs no other tree for pollination.

The dwarf pomegranate has several cultivars from which to choose. Among them are 'Multiplex' with double, creamy white blooms; 'Chico' with double, orange-red

Culture Pomegranates grow naturally in the limestone soil of southeastern Europe, but they are adaptable to the acid soil of the South. Plants are extremely drought tolerant and require very little fertilizer. Just a bit of slow-release fertilizer in spring might spur more vigorous growth, but it is not necessary. Plants grow well in shade or full sun, but flowering is better in full sun. The plants are very adaptable to pruning and can even be sheared into square forms or balls.

Pyracantha coccinea
Firethorn

Say: py-ra-KAN-tha kok-SIN-ee-uh
Salt tolerance: Moderate
Size: 10–18 ft. tall/12–18 ft. wide
Origin: Italy to Caucasus

Hardiness: USDA Zones 5–9
Family: Rosaceae (Rose)
Other name: Scarlet firethorn
Propagation: Seeds; cuttings

Culture Plant firethorn in full sun for best fruiting. Soil should be well drained and infertile. Fertile soil produces rampant growth, which is more susceptible to fireblight. Plants are very drought tolerant. The two most serious diseases of firethorn are fireblight and scab. Plants may also be affected by twig blight, leaf blight, and root rot. Insects such as aphids, lace bugs, and scale insects may be problematic.

Firethorn is a semievergreen to evergreen shrub armed with stiff, thorny branches. White flowers about one-third of an inch in diameter are borne in clusters that literally cover the plant. The fruit is a colorful orange-red berry that ripens in fall and persists into winter.

Firethorn is best used in large-scale places where it has plenty of room to grow and will not be near foot traffic. It is popular for espaliers on walls and trellises, and it is sometimes chosen as an informal hedge or barrier plant. Colorful fruit is its most outstanding attribute.

Fruit can be made into an excellent jelly, and berries are attractive to large birds. Cut branches and stems are popular in Christmas decorations and floral designs.

Several cultivars of *Pyracantha coccinea* are available. In addition, there are at least four other species, which include *P. angustifolia* (narrowleaf firethorn), *P. fortuneana* (Chinese firethorn), *P. koidzummi* (Formosa firethorn), and *P. crenulata* (Nepalese white thorn). Crosses between these species have resulted in many cultivars, some of which are more disease resistant than either parent. Some of the most disease-resistant cultivars are 'Apache', 'Fiery Cascade', 'Mohave', 'Navajo', 'Pueblo', 'Rutgers', 'Shawnee', and 'Teton'. They vary in size and fruit color.

Rhaphiolepis indica
Indian Hawthorn

Say: raff-fee-oh-LEPP-iss IN-dih-kuh
Salt tolerance: High
Size: 3–7 ft. tall/6–10 ft. wide
Origin: India, Southern China

Hardiness: USDA Zones 7B–9B
Family: Rosaceae (Rose)
Other name: Yeddo hawthorn
Propagation: Seeds; cuttings

R. indica

R. umbellata

to diseases such as Entomosporium leafspot. Tiny, circular, bright red spots on both the upper and lower surfaces of young leaves are the first sign of the disease. Large, purple to maroon blotches may develop in advanced stages. If this disease gets a foothold, the plants may become defoliated and eventually die. Root rot is problematic if soil is not well drained. Fireblight may cause whole plants to die. Scale insects and nematodes may cause damage.

Rhaphiolepis umbellata is a larger-growing species. Cultivars 'Majestic Beauty' and 'Rosalinda' top out at about 12 feet. Confusion exists over whether many cultivars are of *Rhaphlolepis indica* or *R. umbellata.* In reality, many familiar cultivars seem to be a hybrid of both species (*Rhaphiolepis ×delacourii*).

Culture Choose a disease-resistant cultivar. Plant in well-drained soil in full sun and provide good air circulation around plants. Prune after flowering, if desired, for compact growth. Fertilize in spring with all-purpose fertilizer, but do not water or fertilize any more than necessary. Excessive new growth makes the plants more susceptible to diseases. Avoid overhead irrigation and be sure that foliage stays as dry as possible.

Indian hawthorn is an attractive, rounded, evergreen plant. In spring, clusters of small, white or pink flowers bloom at the ends of the stalks, literally covering the plants in fragrant blossoms. In fall and winter the plants are decorated with dark berries. Leaves are leathery, evergreen, and two to three inches long.

Indian hawthorn is susceptible

Azalea

Say: roh-do-DEN-dron
Salt tolerance: None
Size: 1–15 ft. tall/1–15 ft. wide
Origin: China, Japan, United States
Hardiness: USDA Zones 6–9

Family: Ericaceae (Heath)
Other name: Honeysuckle (native species)
Propagation: Seeds; cuttings; layering

R. 'Formosa' (Southern Indica type)

Florida flame azalea

Several species of deciduous azaleas are native to North America, but most evergreen azaleas hail from Japan. Over 10,000 different azaleas have been named. A wide variety of plant habits, sizes, colors, and bloom times are available to meet almost any landscaping need or personal preference.

While many small-leafed rhododendrons look like azaleas, there are ways to distinguish between them. Most rhododendron flowers have ten or more stamens, and most azalea flowers have only five or six. Close inspection of the underside of a leaf with a magnifying glass will reveal the true identity; rhododendron leaves are always covered with scales, but azalea leaves never have scales.

Most azaleas bloom in mid-April to mid-May in the mid-Atlantic area of the United States. A few kinds bloom a month or so earlier, but others wait as late as August and September to put on their flowers. Blooms usually last for one or two weeks. Some selections bloom in spring and again in fall. This reblooming trait was used to advantage in the recently introduced Encore™ azaleas.

'Red Ruffles' Rutherfordiana hybrid

Culture Moderate temperatures, slightly acid, well-drained, organic soil and high shade are conditions preferred by most azaleas. If soil is well prepared and azaleas are kept mulched with organic mulch, very little fertilization is required. Azaleas are shallow-rooted and need supplemental irrigation during droughts. Prune as necessary immediately following the bloom period.

Rose

Say: RO-suh
Salt tolerance: Varies
Size: Varies
Origin: Most temperate parts of the world
Hardiness: All USDA Zones

Family: Rosaceae (Rose)
Other names: Many (depending on species)
Propagation: Seeds; cuttings; layering; grafting

R. banksia

polyantha, grandiflora, floribunda, miniature, English/David Austin, landscape roses

Many gardeners in the South are discovering the pleasures of the landscape roses. Many show good disease and pest resistance, have repeat flowering, and are generally more carefree than some of the others. Such recently introduced selections as 'Flower Carpet', 'Home Run', and 'Knock Out' offer many gardeners renewed hope for success with roses.

So beloved is the rose in the United States that it is the national flower, and four states claim a rose as their state flower. The rose is admired the world over, and centuries of hybridizing have led to a wide range of forms and colors.

So many different kinds of roses are available that entire books have been written on the subject. Although there is no single system of classification, most belong to one of the groups listed below. All groups have climbing forms and shrub forms.

Wild roses: several species and hybrids; those that occur in nature
Old garden roses: alba, gallica, damask, centifolia, moss, China, Portland, Bourbon, noisette, tea, hybrid perpetual, Bermuda mystery, and other miscellaneous
Modern garden roses: hybrid teas,

'Louis Philippe'

Culture For success with roses, choose those that are suited to the climate in which you live, buy healthy plants, plant them properly, and care for their basic needs for water, nutrients, any necessary pest and disease control, and pruning. Consult with rosarians and solicit the recommendations of an extension office to find out which ones do best in your area.

Rosmarinus officinalis
Rosemary

Say: rose-ma-REE-nus oh-fiss-ih-NAH-liss

Salt tolerance: High

Size: 1–6 ft. tall/1–6 ft. wide

Origin: Southern Europe, western Asia

Hardiness: USDA Zones 6–11

Family: Lamiaceae (Mint)

Other names: None

Propagation: Cuttings; layering; seeds possible but seedlings are variable

Rosemary is a fragrant, evergreen shrub with needlelike leaves that are green on top and whitish underneath. Plants can be found that are upright or spreading, and size ranges from groundcover selections six inches tall to shrubs up to six feet tall. Flowers may be white, blue, pink, or lavender. Some hybrids have gold or golden-edged foliage.

'Prostratus' is a low, spreading form of rosemary that is often used as a groundcover. Dense foliage forms a thick carpet. Lilac blue flowers bloom from the axils of the leaves along most of the shoot in early spring and sporadically throughout the summer and fall. Use prostrate rosemary on retaining walls and banks, or in containers or hanging baskets. Cultivars 'Salem' and 'Arp' are more winter hardy than other selections.

Rosemary is included in most herb gardens, for it has both culinary and medicinal uses. Use it to season many meats, especially pork, lamb, and venison. Sprinkle in a few leaves to add a bit of flavor to sauces, barbeques, and biscuits.

Culture Rosemary prefers full sun and well-drained, alkaline soil. Avoid places where the foliage will be wet for long periods of time. Add sand or gravel to heavy clay soil to enhance drainage, and add lime if existing soil is too acid. Rosemary is an excellent choice for gardeners who live by bodies of salt water, for it is tolerant of salt spray. Prune as soon as flowers fade to keep plants compact. Plants are very drought tolerant once established. Fertilize lightly with all-purpose, slow-release fertilizer in spring.

Serissa

Serissa japonica

Say: ser-ISS-uh juh-PON-ih-kuh
Salt tolerance: Unknown
Size: 2–4 ft. tall/2–4 ft. wide
Origin: Asia
Hardiness: USDA Zones 7–9

Family: Rubiaceae (Madder)
Other names: Yellow-rim, snowrose, tree of a thousand stars
Propagation: Softwood or hardwood cuttings

Serissa is a small evergreen to semievergreen, fine-textured shrub. Almost year-round, dainty, white flowers about one-third of an inch wide unfurl from pink buds. Leaves have an unpleasant smell when bruised, hence the Latin name *foetida,* which means "stinking."

Serissa is a favorite bonsai subject. Its fine texture, tiny flowers, and potentially gnarly branches make it ideal. In bonsai, the gray trunk, which tends to get lighter in color with age, and its upright stems, which branch in all directions, are qualities that are utilized and emphasized.

Even though serissa may be sensitive to adverse conditions, it seems to be a hardy, adaptable shrub in some places. One that grows on

the University of Georgia campus has survived -3°F and numerous droughts underneath a large live oak.

Many cultivars are available. 'Pink Snow Rose' has leaves edged with white, and flowers are pale pink. Others are 'Variegata', 'Variegated Pink', 'Pink Mystic', 'Snowflake', 'Snowleaves', 'Mt. Fuji', 'Kyoto', 'White Swan', and 'Sapporo'.

Culture Plant serissa in partial shade or in a place that gets morning sun and afternoon shade. Maintain moisture by watering regularly and mulching well. Serissa does not tolerate stress well and responds to conditions that are too dry, too cold, or otherwise not to its liking by dropping its leaves. Deadhead to prolong blooms and prune after flowering to maintain a dense form.

Spiraea cantoniensis 'Lanceata'
Double Reeves' Spirea

Say: spy-REE-ah kan-toe-nee-EN-sis
Salt tolerance: Slight to none
Size: 4–8 ft. tall/4–8 ft. wide
Origin: China and Japan
Hardiness: USDA Zones 5–9

Family: Rosaceae (Rose)
Other names: Spirea, bridal wreath
Propagation: Cuttings of green
 tip shoots in late spring and
 summer; seeds; division

background. Allow each shrub plenty of room to develop and show its naturally graceful form by allowing about eight feet of growing space. Pests and diseases are not a major concern, although plants can become infested with aphids, leaf rollers, or scale insects. The cultivar 'Lanceata' (double Reeves' spirea) is more prevalent in the South than the species.

Eighty to 100 species of *Spiraea* exist. Vanhouttei spirea (*Spiraea ×vanhouttei*) is frequently grown in the South. Japanese spirea (*S. japonica*) is usually smaller and has pinkish flowers and variously colored leaves. *Spiraea prunifolia* can be found on abandoned home sites where it has bloomed for years. In addition to the species, many hybrids (crosses) are available.

Double Reeves' spirea is a deciduous to semievergreen shrub with graceful, arching branches. In spring, masses of tiny, snow-white flowers are borne in two-inch-wide clusters along the stems. In full bloom, the branches cascade and droop like a fountain. For the remainder of the year, the shrubs are nondescript.

Use double Reeves' spirea as a specimen plant, in a mixed border, or in a mass planting. Flowers display best when planted in front of other green plants or a dark

Culture Plant in full sun for best flowering. Prune immediately after flowering to control growth and to make the plants more compact. Remove individual branches back to the ground to maintain the plant's arching form. Reeves' spirea is not particular about soil, but it should be well drained. Once established, it tolerates neglect and is drought tolerant.

American Snowbell

Say: STY-raks a-mer-ih-KAH-nus
Salt tolerance: None
Size: 6–8 ft. tall/6–8 ft. wide
Origin: Native from Virginia to Florida
west to Missouri, Louisiana, and
east Texas

Hardiness: USDA Zones 5–9
Family: Styraceae (Styrax)
Other names: Mock orange, storax,
American silverbells
Propagation: Seeds (after cold, moist
stratification); softwood cuttings

J. S. Peterson

American snowbell is a deciduous shrub with a widely branched crown. In spring, showy, white, bell-faced flowers with five spreading, recurved petals hang from the leaf axils in clusters of one to four. Fragrant flowers about half an inch long flare out to a width just a bit more or less than an inch, and a white style extends beyond the ten stamens. Round, quarter-inch fruits that follow are attractive to birds and other wildlife.

Use storax in native mixed borders as a very small tree, or let it mature more naturally as a multibranched shrub. Leaves are host to the promethean moth (*Callosamia*

promethean) and the flowers provide nectar for bees, which serve as pollinating insects.

Big-leaf snowbell (*Styrax grandiflora*) has longer flower clusters and larger leaves. It is also native and is hardy in Zones 7–9. Japanese snowbell (*Styrax japonicus*) grows much larger (20–30 feet tall and equal or greater spread), and is a dainty, low-branched tree that is worthy of extensive use in Southern landscapes.

Paul Redfearn

Culture American snowbell grows naturally in rich, damp, poorly drained acid soil. It is normally found in such wet places as swamp margins, stream beds, lake edges, oxbow lakes, and floodplains. Although it flowers most prolifically with a good bit of sun, it is best situated where it will be protected from the full western afternoon sun.

Viburnums

About 250 species of *Viburnums* are included in the Adoxaceae family. Although genetic tests have placed them squarely in this family, some botanists still place them in the family Caprifoliaceae. Viburnums can be found in cold-temperate to semitropical climates in most of the world.

Viburnums are usually shrubs, but some can attain the dimensions of a small tree. A few dwarf varieties are under three feet tall while others can become medium-sized trees up to 30 feet tall. Leaves vary in size, color, and texture. Foliage may be rounded, lobed like a maple leaf, or lance-shaped, and may have entire or toothed edges. On some specimens foliage is smooth and glossy, but on others it may be dull or even velvety or leathery. Foliage on some species is evergreen or semievergreen while on others it is deciduous. Many species have colorful fall foliage.

Individual florets are produced in clusters, usually at the ends of the branches. Five-petaled florets may be white, cream, or pink. The clusters may be flat-topped so that they resemble lacecap hydrangeas, or they may be more rounded and globe- or dome-shaped. Some are fragrant, some give off no fragrance, and some are downright stinky. Some species have showy sterile flowers around the edges of the cluster that surround the less showy fertile flowers, while others may have only sterile flowers. Buds are often shaped like small nuts and add to the attractiveness of the species.

Each fruit, which contains a single seed (drupe), is round, oval, or somewhat flattened and may be yellow, red, orange, pink, purple, blue, or black. Seeds are eaten by birds and other wildlife, and some, though not all, can be eaten by humans. Leaves are the larval food plant of some butterflies and moths, and flowers provide nectar for bees, butterflies, and other insects.

Some viburnums appreciate full sun but will do just as well in light to partial shade, while others prefer a shady site. Most thrive on moderately fertile, moist but well-drained soil with a slightly acid pH (5.5–6.5). When sited properly and given adequate space for good air circulation, viburnums are seldom bothered by pests or diseases.

In this genus can be found many versatile and garden-worthy subjects. Choose from among them for showy flowers, fruit, and colorful fall foliage. Many are great in mixed borders, where they are well behaved and stay put. Others sucker and form colonies; some become invasive and displace other species. A colonizing species might be a good choice for a natural area where a group of plants is desired. However, if a specimen is wanted for a formal landscape, it might be wise to select one that does not sucker readily.

Most viburnums are not self-pollinating. Except for *V. opulus,* they are self-incompatible, which means that they need some genetic variability to fruit well. Three cuttings of the same plant (clones) might not cross-pollinate, but three seedlings with some genetic variations would be good companions that would most likely result in a heavy fruit set.

The list that follows is not by any means a complete listing of all viburnums that will do well in the South. Frequently, determining the correct species is difficult, as there are several 'snowball' flowering types as well as some hybrids of complex ancestry. Even the experts have not finally settled on the correct name for all the species. With a bit of study and consideration, a good decision can be made regarding which of the viburnums would best fit your landscape.

A Roundup of Viburnums for the South

Viburnum acerifolium
Mapleleaf viburnum

Say: vy-BUR-num a-ser-ih-FOH-lee-um

Origin: Eastern United States from New Brunswick south to North Carolina and Georgia

Flowers: Flat-topped clusters of yellowish-white flowers

Fruit: Almost black

Hardiness: USDA Zones 3–8

Size: 3–6 ft. tall/3–4 ft. wide

Comments: Shade tolerant; suckers to form loose, open colonies in the wild; adapted to shade and dry soil; host of butterflies and attractive to birds; leaves three-lobed like a maple; foliage deciduous, turning reddish-purple in fall; tolerates deep shade and dry soil

V. acerifolium

Viburnum awabuki
Awabuki sweet viburnum

Say: vy-BUR-num aw-wah-BOO-kee

Origin: Korea, Japan, eastern China, Taiwan

Flowers: Fragrant, white

Fruit: Red, but minimally produced because it is self-sterile and requires another seedling or clone for cross-pollination

Hardiness: USDA Zones 7–9

Size: 15–20 ft. tall/15–20 ft. wide

Comments: Sometimes considered a cultivar of *V. odoratissimum;* leaves not foul-smelling like *V. odoratissimum;* very glossy, thick leaves; requires well-drained soil and is drought tolerant; excellent hedge or may be grown into a small tree

Viburnum ×burkwoodii
Burkwood viburnum

Say: vy-BUR-num × berk-WOOD-ee-eye

Origin: Hybrid

Flowers: Pink in bud; white, fragrant snowball

Fruit: Red changing to black; usually sparsely produced

Hardiness: USDA Zones 5–8

Size: 6–12 ft. tall/6–8 ft. wide

Comments: Slow to medium growth; upright, multistemmed habit; excellent choice for shrub border where fragrance permeates the entire garden; pollution and heat tolerant; deciduous to semievergreen; several cultivars

Viburnum cassinoides
Witherod viburnum or swamp blackhaw

Say: vy-BUR-num cass-in-OY-deez
Origin: Newfoundland to Manitoba and Minnesota south to Georgia and Florida
Flowers: Creamy white, flat-topped clusters two to five inches in diameter
Fruit: Green to pink and then red to blue before becoming black; all colors often present
Hardiness: USDA Zones 5–8
Size: 5–12 ft. tall/5–10 ft. wide
Comments: Attractive, dense shrub; emerging leaves often bronze or purple tinted; fall foliage orange, red, and purple; tolerant of coastal conditions; similar to *V. nudum* (possum-haw viburnum) but can be distinguished from it by the toothed leaf margins

Viburnum dentatum
Arrowwood viburnum

Say: vy-BUR-num den-TAY-tum
Origin: Eastern North America
Flowers: Creamy white lacecap clusters about three inches in diameter; unpleasantly scented
Fruit: Deep porcelain-blue to blue-purple
Hardiness: USDA Zones 2–8
Size: 6–12 ft. tall/6–12 ft. wide
Comments: Deciduous shrub or understory tree; grows wild in woodlands, bogs, and along stream banks but is urban tolerant; adapts to varied soil conditions; fruit attractive to many birds; several cultivars; medium-sized to large; upright, oval form in youth becoming arching, spreading, and suckering with age; used by Indians for arrow shafts; tolerant of heat, cold, and alkaline soil

Viburnum japonicum
Japanese viburnum

Say: vy-BUR-num ja-PON-ih-kum
Origin: Japan
Flowers: White clusters three to four and one-half inches in diameter; fragrant
Fruit: Red, oval to rounded
Hardiness: USDA Zones 7–9
Size: 6–10 ft. tall/6–10 ft. wide
Comments: Extremely dense, good screen; shade tolerant in Southeast; leathery, glossy evergreen leaves; some hybrid species have this as one of the parents; similar to and often confused with *V. odoratissimum* and *V. awabuki*

V. ×juddii
Judd viburnum

Say: vy-BUR-num × JUD-ee-eye
Origin: Hybrid of *V. carlesii* and *V. bitchiuense*
Flowers: White intensely fragrant semisnowball-shaped cluster opening from crimson buds
Fruit: Red ripening to black
Hardiness: USDA Zones 4–8
Size: 6–10 ft. tall/6–10 ft. wide
Comments: Rounded habit; deciduous

Viburnum macrocephalum
Chinese snowball viburnum

Say: vy-BUR-num mak-roh-SEF-uh-lum
Origin: China
Flowers: White, nonfragrant balls of blooms three to eight inches in diameter; very showy; florets first apple green and then white
Fruit: Does not fruit, as flowers are sterile

a snowball type

Hardiness: USDA Zones 6–9
Size: 6–15+ ft. tall/6–15 ft. wide
Comments: Semievergreen foliage in the South; tends to flower a second time in fall

Viburnum nudum
Smooth witherod
Say: vy-BUR-num NEW-doom
Origin: Eastern United States
Flowers: Small, creamy white, flat-topped clusters
Fruit: Starts out green and then turns pink, rose, bluish, and finally midnight blue
Hardiness: USDA Zones 5–9
Size: 6–12 ft. tall/5–10 ft. wide
Comments: Most frequently a multibranched deciduous shrub with very glossy foliage and variably colored fall foliage. Usually found along stream and river banks or in swamps and swamp borders; several cultivars; endangered or threatened in some states

Viburnum obovatum
Walter viburnum, small viburnum
Say: vy-BUR-num ob-oh-VAY-tum
Origin: South Carolina, through central Florida, to Alabama along the coastal plain
Flowers: Creamy white, flat-topped clusters two to three inches in diameter
Fruit: Green maturing to pink, red, burgundy, purplish-blue, and then purplish-black
Hardiness: USDA Zones 6–9
Size: 6–15 + ft. tall/6–15 ft. wide
Comments: Evergreen in mild winters; dense, twiggy growth great for hedges, screens, and wildlife habitat; several cultivars; grows naturally in moist to wet soil in full sun to partial shade but will acclimate to drier soil once established; remove root suckers in formal garden situations or allow to colonize in natural areas; distinguish from holly species by alternately placed leaves of holly

Viburnum odoratissimum
Sweet viburnum
Say: vy-BUR-num oh-duh-ruh-TISS-ih-mum
Origin: Asia
Flowers: Conical clusters of small white fragrant flowers
Fruit: Berries that turn from red to black; sparingly produced
Hardiness: USDA Zones 8–10
Size: 10–20+ ft. tall/8–15 ft. wide
Comments: Large shrub or small tree; evergreen; great for screening; can be limbed up for a standard; salt tolerant and adaptable to full sun or partial shade; leaves release a fetid odor when crushed; not as hardy as V. awabuki, but sometimes confused with it

Viburnum opulus
European cranberrybush viburnum
Say: vi-BUR-num OP-yoo-lus
Origin: Europe, northern Africa, and northern Asia
Flowers: White; outer ring of showy sterile flowers with inner ring of fertile, inconspicuous flowers; lacecap type
Fruit: Bright red persisting into winter and drying up like a raisin
Hardiness: USDA Zones 3–8
Size: 8–12 ft. tall/10–15 ft. wide
Comments: Upright, spreading, with branches arching to the ground; considered invasive in Pennsylvania, Indiana, and Wisconsin; several garden-worthy cultivars, including 'Roseum' the European snowball or Guelder-rose, with extremely showy, sterile flowers, often seen around older residences; aphid infestations problematic

Viburnum prunifolium
Blackhaw viburnum
Say: vy-BUR-num proo-ni-FOH-lee-um
Origin: Eastern, Southern, and Midwestern United States
Flowers: Creamy white lacecap clusters
Fruit: Mixture of green, yellow, and red changing to bluish-black with a waxy gray bloom
Hardiness: USDA Zones 3–9
Size: 12–15+ ft. tall/ 8–12 ft. wide
Comments: Deciduous; purple-red fall foliage; prefers dry sites but can adapt to wet soil; adapts to sun or shade; good substitute for crabapples; fruit makes good jelly; attractive to wildlife; small tree to large shrub; upright, oval form in youth becoming upright and rounded with age; urban tolerant; often suckers and forms thickets

Viburnum rhytidophyllum
Leatherleaf viburnum
Say: vy-BUR-num ry-ti-do-FIL-um
Origin: Central and western China
Flowers: Four- to eight-inch, yellowish-white, flat-topped clusters (cymes); slightly fragrant
Fruit: Red, ripening to glossy black
Hardiness: USDA Zones 6–8
Size: 10–15 ft. tall/10–15 ft. wide
Comments: Vigorous and fast-growing; adaptable to wide variety of soils; boldly textured evergreen shrub with large leaves four to eight inches long and one to two and one-half inches wide.

Viburnum rufidulum
Southern blackhaw viburnum, rusty black-haw
Say: vy-BUR-num roo-FID-yoo-lum
Origin: Southern United States
Flowers: White lacecap; buds covered with deep, rich, rusty brown pubescence
Fruit: Dark blue but requires cross-pollination with a seedling (not a cutting or clone) for fruit production
Hardiness: USDA Zones 5–9
Size: 10–20 ft. tall/10–15 ft. wide
Comments: Deciduous small tree with colorful fall foliage; larger and more open in shade; easily trained to a standard; occurs naturally in upland, well-drained woods, so is drought tolerant once established

Viburnum suspensum
Sandankwa viburnum
Say: vy-BUR-num sus-PEN-sum
Origin: Okinawa and other Ryukyu Islands
Flowers: Waxy white with pinkish tint in clusters about two and one-half to four inches long and wide
Fruit: Red maturing to black
Hardiness: USDA Zones 8–11
Size: 6–12 ft. tall/6–12 ft. wide
Comments: Great for medium-height trimmed hedges; good for landscapes in the Coastal Plain; frequently used in Florida gardens

Viburnum tinus
Laurestinus
Say: vy-BUR-num TIN-us
Origin: Southern Europe, northern Africa
Flowers: Pink buds open to white flower clusters two to four inches in diameter; slightly fragrant
Fruit: Ovoid, metallic-blue fruits maturing to black
Hardiness: USDA Zones 7–10
Size: 6–12 ft. tall/5–10 ft. wide
Comments: Glossy evergreen leaves attractive throughout the year; moderately salt tolerant; excellent for screening and hedging; several cultivars

Viburnum tinus

Weigela florida
Weigela

Say: wy-GEE-la FLOR-id-uh
Salt tolerance: Slight
Size: 6–9 ft. tall/9–12 ft. wide
Origin: Japan

Hardiness: USDA Zones 4–8
Family: Diervillaceae (Teasel)
Other names: None
Propagation: Cuttings; seeds

Weigela is a large deciduous shrub with a spreading, rounded habit. Branches often arch to the ground with age. In late spring or early summer, one-inch, funnel- to bell-shaped flowers bloom in such profusion that the entire shrub seems covered with them. Old-fashioned weigela blossoms are typically rosy pink on the outside and paler on the inside. Cultivars and hybrids can be found with flowers of red, white, salmon, and combinations of these colors. Many display yellow or golden throats. Fruit is a smooth, two-valved capsule about one inch long that has no ornamental value.

The shrub's botanical name has nothing to do with the state of Florida. Florida, in fact, means "flowering," so the appellation refers to the plant's abundant flowers. Weigela offers no significant fall color, and it can be coarse and unattractive in winter. It is best planted in a shrub border where other shrubs can mask its unsightliness in winter.

So many hybrids and cultivars are known that it would take considerable space to list them all. Plants can be selected for various characteristics. Many flower colors are available. Leaf color may be various shades of green or yellow with purple or red tinges, or they may be variegated and contain a combination of colors.

Proven Winners

Culture Plant weigela in full sun to partial shade. While adaptable to a wide range of soils, well-drained soil is important to its welfare. Prune to shape after the plant has finished flowering. Frequent dieback of limbs may require considerable pruning. No serious disease or insect problems are of big concern, and the plant is pollution tolerant.

Yucca filamentosa
Adam's Needle

Say: YUK-uh fil-uh-men-TOH-suh
Salt tolerance: High
Size: 3–15 ft. tall/3–4 ft. wide
Origin: Southeastern United States
Hardiness: USDA Zones 4–9

Family: Agavaceae (Agave)
Other name: Bear grass
Propagation: Seeds; root cuttings; removal of offshoots

Adam's needle has evergreen, swordlike leaves about one inch wide that taper to a sharp point. Stiffly erect, the leaves form a rosette as they emerge from hidden underground stems. Along the margins of the leaves are long, curly threads, or filaments. In summer, a tall spike emerges. At the top of the spike is a very showy cluster (panicle) of flowers with up to several dozen down-hanging, two-inch-long, white flowers. Fruit capsules contain from 120 to 150 seeds that are dispersed by the wind.

If you are lucky enough to have bear grass in an appropriate place in your landscape, let it be. It is a durable, drought tolerant native that will survive with no help from the gardener. If you have more than you need, or want to clear an area of bear grass, you may have a problem. Long tap roots are almost impossible to dig up. New plants grow readily from any root pieces that remain in the ground.

Some experts consider *Yucca flaccida, Y. smalliana,* and *Y. concava* as separate species, but others group them together under *Y. filamentosa.* Several cultivars are available. 'Golden Sword' has stripes of gold variegation down the center of each leaf. 'Color Guard' is similarly colored but has more crisply defined gold stripes. 'Bright Edge' has green leaves with thin but prominent yellow margins. 'Gold Garland' has gold variegation when it is young that transforms to green as the leaf matures. 'Ivory' has cream-colored variegation, and 'Hofer Blue' is blue-silver to blue-green in spring, fading to green-blue in winter.

Culture Grow Adam's needle on dry, sandy, or rocky soil. Place plants about three feet apart and water well until established. Cut down spent bloom spikes, as they are unsightly but will persist for two or three years. Plants will die after flowering, but new plants will emerge from lateral buds produced by the "mother" plant. Plants are tolerant of heat, drought, blazing sun, and salt spray.

Yucca gloriosa
Spanish Dagger

Say: YUK-uh glo-ree-OH-suh
Salt tolerance: High
Size: 3–15 ft. tall/3–4 ft. wide
Origin: Southeastern United States
Hardiness: USDA Zones 7–11
Family: Agavaceae (Agave)

Other names: Palm lily, mound-lily yucca
Propagation: Seeds; rooted cuttings taken in winter; offsets taken in spring; cut branches

margins. The yuccas are pollinated only by a specific species of moths (yucca moths).

Flowers, fruits, roots, and stems are edible. Flowers are tasty raw or cooked, and the stems can be used like asparagus. The roots can be cooked or dried and ground into a powder that can be used to make bread. Ropes, cloth, baskets, and mats are made from a fiber obtained from the leaves. Roots are sometimes used as a soap substitute.

Spanish dagger is an evergreen shrub with rigid, swordlike leaves about two inches wide and two to three feet long. The grayish-green leaves originate from a basal rosette, and they have smooth margins and pointed tips. In late summer Spanish dagger blooms with showy, fragrant, white, pendulous flowers that are held in an erect cluster (panicle) above the terminal leaves. Plants stay in a stemless clump for several years, but with age a trunk or stem may develop and lift the leaves as high as six to eight feet.

Spanish dagger is a gentler plant than its cousins *Yucca filamentosa* (Adam's needle) and *Y. aloifolia* (Spanish bayonet) because the needle tips are not as sharp. The cultivar 'Mobilis' has dark green leaves, and 'Variegata' has leaves with yellow

Culture Plant Spanish dagger in full sun and sandy, well-drained soil. Tolerant of a range of pH as well as salt, it is a good choice for seaside plantings. Pest and disease problems are usually minimal. Leaf spot may be problematic in areas with poor air circulation. Although plants are very cold hardy, winter dampness and prolonged snow may cause decay. Yucca moth larvae may bore into the terminal shoot and weaken it. In places where this moth is not present, viable seed will not be produced without hand pollination. Scale insects can be troublesome. Individual crowns die after flowering, but new side shoots are produced so that plants are always present. Never remove specimens from the wild, as they are endangered in part of their range.

Chapter 3

Herbaceous
or Semiwoody Shrubs

These shrubs were included because of their value to Southern landscapes. In parts of the South where freezing weather seldom visits, they may be evergreen. In areas where freezes are likely, they perform much as herbaceous perennials. In locations where they are not hardy at all, they can be planted in containers and moved to protected places during the winter. Their beauty in the landscape is such that they can even be grown as annuals and replaced each spring.

The firebush *(Hamelia patens)* will bloom throughout the summer and attract hummingbirds to the landscape.

Barleria cristata
Philippine Violet

Say: bar-LEER-ee-uh kriss-TAY-tuh
Salt tolerance: Slight
Size: 4–6 ft. tall/3–4 ft. wide
Origin: India, Myanmar
Hardiness: USDA Zones 8–11

Family: Acanthaceae (Acanthus)
Other names: Bluebell barleria, barleria
Propagation: Seeds; cuttings (easy)

blue form

white form

All spring and summer the dark green foliage of barleria provides an attractive backdrop for other colorful flowers. In fall, when many of the summer-flowering plants begin looking bedraggled, barleria's fresh and cool blue or white funnel-shaped flowers are a welcome addition to the landscape. The first frost usually puts an end to the show, but the roots are hardy in Zone 8 and south. Expect it to resprout in the spring.

Expect to find volunteer seedlings in the landscape. Pull them or pot them up to share with friends. Sometimes barleria can become weedy and escape into areas where it is not wanted. Be aware that it is listed as an invasive species in Hawaii and other tropical areas. The University of Florida Institute of Food and Agricultural Sciences (IFAS) says that there is not a problem with invasiveness in Florida at this time, and that it can be recommended by IFAS faculty.

Another species, *Barleria involucrata,* is similar except that flowers and leaves are larger and the flower color is blue lilac.

Culture Barleria appreciates full sun to partial shade and well-drained soil. No pests are of major concern, but a leaf spot disease may be problematic. The plants are very drought tolerant. Cut back to the ground after the frost kills the tops and mulch well to protect the crown. Leaves are coarse and sandpapery after they have been subjected to freezing weather, and the brown seeds are somewhat prickly, so wear gloves when you work around them.

Brugmansia spp.
Angel's Trumpet

Say: brug-MAN-see-uh
Salt tolerance: Moderate/Slight
Size: 6–15 ft. tall/6–20 ft. wide
Origin: Subtropical regions of South America

Hardiness: USDA Zones 8–11
Family: Solanaceae (Nightshade)
Other names: Brugs, brugmansia, angel-star
Propagation: Seeds; cuttings (easy)

Culture Brugmansias prefer moist, fertile, well-drained soil in full sun to partial shade. They do best with humid, warm days (80–85ºF) and cool nights (no less than 40ºF). The tops of the plants will be killed by freezing weather. The plants are root hardy, however, and will resprout in spring. They may even survive the winter in USDA Zones 7 and lower if their roots are well mulched. Pests such as caterpillars, aphids, mealy bugs, and spider mites may be troublesome.

Brugmansias, affectionately called "brugs" by aficionados, grow and bloom year-round in frost-free areas. They produce spectacular pendulous, funnel- or trumpet-shaped flowers in shades of white, yellow, gold, orange, peach, or pink. Blossoms may be double, triple, or quadruple, or shredded. Some of the giant bells hang straight down while others (nodding) may stick out to the side. Fruits (seed pods) may be shaped like okra pods, chili peppers, green beans, or eggs, and they never have bumps or spines as some of the *Daturas* do. The flowers are fragrant, especially in the early evenings.

Seven species of *Brugmansia* have been identified, and they are divided into the *B. aurea* group (*aurea, insignis, suaveolens,* and *versicolor*) and the *B. arborea* group (*arborea, sanguinea,* and *vulcanicola*). The two groups normally do not cross with each other.

Closely related to the *Brugmansias* and sharing the angel's trumpet name is the genus *Datura.* However, *Datura* is herbaceous and the flowers are held face up, while Brugmansia is a woody perennial with pendulous flowers.

All parts of *Datura* and *Brugmansia* are highly toxic and should not be ingested.

Brunfelsia pauciflora
Yesterday Today and Tomorrow

Say: brun-FELZ-ee-uh paw-
  see-FLOR-uh
Salt tolerance: Moderate
Size: 3–8 ft. tall/2–5 ft. wide
Origin: Brazil
Hardiness: USDA Zones 8B–11

Family: Solanaceae (Nightshade)
Other names: Morning-noon-and-
  night, Brazilian raintree
Propagation: Tip cuttings of new
  growth; seeds; suckers

Yesterday today and tomorrow is spectacular in bloom. Flowers open dark purple and then turn pale lavender and finally white. Reminiscent of pansies, the two-inch-diameter tubular flowers literally cover the plant. Some species bloom most of the summer, but others bloom for two or three weeks in spring. This shortcoming is of minor concern, for little can compare to its beauty when it is in full bloom. In Zone 8 the plant loses some of its leaves in the winter, but it is evergreen farther south.

Brunfelsia is a genus of about 40 species of shrubs and small trees. *Brunfelsia pauciflora* 'Floribunda Compacta' grows about four feet tall, and it blooms for two or three weeks in spring. New plants sprout around the plant from suckers, which are easy to pot up and share with friends.

Several cultivars of *B. pauciflora* are in the trade. 'Eximia' is the one most commonly cultivated. 'Floribunda Compacta' is smaller but less frequently planted than 'Floribunda', while 'Macrantha' has larger flowers but is less hardy than the species. *Brunfelsia americana* is the tropical lady-of-the-night that releases its considerable fragrance in the evening.

Like many members of the nightshade family, *Brunfelsia* contains poisonous substances. The berries are extremely toxic, and all parts of the plant (flowers, leaves, berries, and seeds) should be considered toxic to animals. Dogs appear to be particularly attracted to the berries and seeds.

Culture *Brunfelsia* does well in full sun to partial shade and appreciates a bit of protection from the hot afternoon sun. Moist, well-drained, slightly acid soil enriched with organic matter suits it well. Blooms are produced on the tips of new growth, so pruning to encourage branching increases the number of flowers. Grow in a container and move to a protected place in winter if temperatures regularly fall below 30°F.

Cestrum aurantiacum
Yellow Cestrum

Say: SES-trum aw-ran-ti-AYE-kum
Salt tolerance: Moderate
Size: 7–10 ft. tall/3–5 ft. wide
Origin: Guatemala
Hardiness: USDA Zones 8B–11

Family: Solanaceae (Nightshade)
Other names: Orange cestrum, gold jasmine, yellow shrub jessamine
Propagation: Cuttings; seeds

place during the winter. The tubular flowers are attractive to butterflies and hummingbirds. Foliage smells like a wet dog if the leaves are touched.

Other species of *Cestrum* include red cestrum (*C. elegans*), which has red flowers and berries; green cestrum (*C. parqui*); and the intensely fragrant night-blooming jasmine (*C. nocturnum*). It is interesting to note that red, yellow, and green cestrum are invasive in Australia.

The Solanaceae family includes some of our most well-known plants, including potatoes, tomatoes,

eggplant, sweet peppers, tobacco, and petunias. Some members of the family have medicinal value, and some are quite poisonous.

Selected in 2000 as a Florida Plant of the Year by the Florida Nursery Growers and Landscape Association, this plant stands out in the summer garden. Clusters of tubular, dark yellow flowers borne in axillary and terminal clusters are often so profuse that the limbs are bent down. Flowers are followed by small, white berries that are relished by birds and stand out well in contrast to deep green leaves. Although evergreen in tropical areas, it gets killed to the ground by frost.

This woody shrub usually gets killed to the ground in north Florida, but it recovers nicely in spring. In places with very severe winter temperatures, it can be grown in a container and moved to a protected

Culture Yellow cestrum prefers full to partial sun and well-drained, loamy soil. Water regularly until the plant is well established and then only as needed. A general purpose fertilizer can be applied before new growth begins in spring. Prune after the plant blooms to shape, if needed.

Clerodendrum paniculatum
Pagoda Flower

Say: kler-oh-DEN-drum pan-ick-yoo-LAY-tum
Salt tolerance: Slight
Size: 3–5 ft. tall/2–3 ft. wide
Origin: India, Sri Lanka, Malaysia, and much of southeastern Asia

Hardiness: USDA Zones 8–11
Family: Lamiaceae (Mint)
Other names: None
Propagation: Division of suckers; cuttings

Pagoda flower in its tropical habitat is an erect, open, semiwoody, evergreen shrub. In summer showy clusters of orange-red flowers are held above the foliage. The common name comes from the fact that the cluster is shaped like a Japanese pagoda.

Each individual funnel-shaped flower is small, but the large terminal cluster (panicle) contains hundreds of flowers and may be up to one foot or more in height. Multiple stamens protrude from each five-petaled trumpet, and a papery, peach-colored, petal-like outer whorl adds an interesting two-tone effect.

Cultivars of *C. paniculatum* include 'Alba', which has green and white flowers, and 'Borneo Sunset', which has reddish-purple leaves.

Some members of the *Clerodendrum* genus have a tendency to become invasive in the garden. While pagoda flower does produce numerous suckers, most gardeners do not consider it invasive because the suckers tend to stay in the immediate area of the mother plant and do not spread out in the garden aggressively. Individual shrubs are relatively short-lived, so new plants are usually welcome.

Clerodendrum is a genus of about 400 species. Others commonly grown in Southern gardens are *C. bungei* (Cashmere bouquet), *C. speciosissimum* (Java glorybower), *C. quadriloculare* (fireworks plant), *C. thomsoniae* (bleeding heart glorybower), and *C. trichotomum* (Harlequin glorybower).

Culture Pagoda flower appreciates a fertile and moist but well-drained soil. Regular applications of a balanced fertilizer during the growing season will keep it vigorous. Flowering will be best in full sun, but partial shade is tolerated. In Zone 8 it gets killed to the ground in winter unless it is protected from freezing weather, but it resprouts in spring. Plants grown in large containers will do well in colder zones if moved inside during the winter.

Cuphea spp.
Cuphea

Say: KOO-fee-uh or KYOO-fee-uh
Salt tolerance: Slight to none
Size: See each entry below
Origin: Warm temperate and tropical regions of the Americas
Hardiness: Zones 8–11
Family: Lythraceae (Loosestrife)

Members of the *Cuphea* genus are woody-stemmed perennials or subshrubs. They bloom best in full sun, have few pests, and are drought and heat tolerant. Cupheas are evergreen in the tropics; in Zone 8 they get killed to the ground by freezing weather, but most resprout from hardy roots in spring. All cupheas are attractive to hummingbirds, butterflies, and bees. Propagation is easy from tip cuttings.

C. ignea (IG-nee-uh)
3–4 ft. tall/3–4 ft. wide
Common name: Cigar plant, cigarette plant, firecracker plant, cigar flower
Narrow, one-inch-long, tubular, red-orange flowers with yellow tips suggest a tiny lit cigar.

C. llavea (LAH-vay-uh)
1–2 ft. tall/3–4 ft. wide
Common name: Bat-face cuphea, tiny mice cuphea, bunny's ears, St. Peter's plant
Masses of one-inch, tubular, purple flowers lipped with two upward-facing red petals bloom throughout the summer. The flowers resemble tiny bats' faces.

C. micropetala (my-kro-PET-uh-luh)
5–6 ft. tall/3–4 ft. wide
Common name: Tall cigar plant, candy corn plant
Tubular flowers open creamy yellow, but as they age, the base turns orange-red and then the entire flower takes on that color. Blooms are produced when the days shorten in fall.

C. hyssopifolia (hiss-sop-ih-FOH-lee-uh)   1–2 ft. tall/2–3 ft. wide
Common name: Mexican heather, false heather, Hawaiian heather, elfin herb
Very fine, flat sprays of foliage on densely branched stems and tiny lavender, pink, or white flowers are the distinguishing marks of this cuphea.

C. varia (VAR-ee-uh)
1–3 ft. tall/2–3 ft. wide
Common name: Pink cigar, pink Cuphea, 'Susan's Little Gem' (a popular cultivar)
Flowers of this species are varied and range from white to lavender and pink. Tubular flowers have six widely spaced petals that radiate out from the edges of the tube.

Others: *C. procumbens, C. purpurea, C. rosea, C. cyanea*

Duranta erecta
Golden Dewdrop

Say: door-AN-tuh ee-RECK-tuh
Salt tolerance: Moderate to Slight
Size: 8–15 ft. tall/10–15 ft. wide
Origin: Tropical America; south
   Florida and south Texas
   (possibly naturalized)
Hardiness: USDA Zones 8B–11

Family: Verbenaceae (Verbena)
Other names: Brazilian sky flower,
   duranta, pigeon berry, sky
   flower
Propagation: Easy from tip cuttings;
   seeds

reaches of its hardiness range, it does not attain the stature of plants growing in the tropics. It is an attractive annual in zones farther north.

Use in mixed shrub borders or as an attractive specimen. Several cultivars are available, including the variegated forms 'Variegata' and 'Golden Edge'. 'Alba' has white flowers and 'Sapphire Showers' has violet-blue, ruffled flowers with narrow, white picotee edges. Flowers attract butterflies, and the berries are attractive to birds but poisonous to humans.

The flowers and fruit of golden dewdrop are its chief attributes. Throughout the summer, blue flowers hang in loose, six-inch-long clusters, and they are followed by half-inch, showy yellow to yellow-orange elongated spherical to teardrop-shaped fruits.

Duranta is a spreading plant with branches that are sometimes droopy and vinelike. Plants growing in the wild may have thorns, but those that are nursery grown are usually thornless. In USDA Zones 8B and 9, it gets killed to the ground most winters but returns with vigor the following year. In the northern

Culture Golden dewdrop blooms best in full sun but is satisfactory in partial shade. It tolerates soil that is slightly alkaline or acid and needs moderate fertility and moisture-retentive but well-drained soil. Prune while small to make a more compact shrub and to improve shape. In areas where it does not get killed to the ground in winter, it may become aggressive.

Galphimia glauca
Thryallis

Say: gal-FIM-ee-uh GLAW-kuh
Salt tolerance: Moderate
Size: 5–7 ft. tall/4–6 ft. wide
Origin: Tropical areas from Mexico to Guatemala
Hardiness: USDA Zones 8B–11

Family: Malpighiaceae (Malpighia)
Other names: Rain-of-gold, golden shower
Propagation: Softwood cuttings in summer; seeds sown while still green

tropics, where it blooms year-round. Elsewhere, it can be used as a patio plant or as seasonal color in perennial or shrub borders. In areas where it gets killed to the ground, it is a late summer and fall bloomer. A period of cool weather will cause the leaves to take on bronze tones.

Throughout the summer in tropical areas, thryallis blooms with three-quarter-inch yellow blossoms held in clusters at the tips of stems. Flowers are followed by three-part seed capsules. The dense foliage is comprised of short-stalked, one- to two-inch, light green, oblong leaves that seem to be dusted with a light frosting. Slender stems are covered with red hairs.

Extremely brittle branches have caused some people to call it ice plant, because it shatters like a thin sheet of ice tapped with a teaspoon. Take this into consideration when placing the plant in the landscape, and make sure that it is protected from rambunctious pets and ball-chasing children. Although *Galphimia glauca* and *G. gracilis* are both listed as species in the APG II 2003 system, most references treat them as synonyms.

Thryallis makes an excellent hedge or specimen plant in the

Culture Thryallis grows best in full sun and in fertile, moist, well-drained soil. Well-established shrubs are moderately drought tolerant. Regular pruning helps keep the plants compact and attractive and encourages continued flowering. Regular fertilizer applications result in more vigorous growth. No consequential problems with insects and diseases are evident.

Hamelia patens
Firebush

Say: ham-EE-lee-uh PAT-ens
Salt tolerance: Moderate
Size: 8–12 ft. tall/8–12 ft. wide
Origin: Mexico, south Florida, the West Indies, and Central and South America

Hardiness: USDA Zones 8–11
Family: Rubiaceae (Madder)
Other names: Mexican firebush, firecracker shrub, scarlet bush
Propagation: Softwood cuttings in spring; fresh seeds

Hamelia patens 'Compacta'

Culture Firebush is one of our heat-loving plants. Thriving in full sun, it is a long-season, low-maintenance shrub. Although firebush is drought tolerant, it responds well to regular watering and a light fertilization in spring. Extremely insect and disease tolerant, the bush remains a picture of robust health throughout the summer.

Firebush is a standout in fall gardens. All summer long it grows and blooms, but late summer is its showiest season. For months it has produced terminal clusters of bright reddish-orange tubular flowers, and then in fall the leaves turn red. Even the flower stems are red, and clusters of fruit ripening in the midst of all this color makes quite a striking display.

In its native habitat, firebush is an evergreen shrub that blooms most of the year, and it grows into a large shrub or small tree. In most of the South, however, it gets killed to the ground by frost and must start over each year. North of I-10, it is usually grown as an annual.

Hummingbirds and butterflies admire this garden workhorse. In 1998 it was listed by the Florida Nursery Growers and Landscape Association as a Florida Plant of the Year. A dwarf version, *Hamelia patens* 'Compacta', might be more suited to small gardens or containers. Golden tubular flowers are held up by bright red stems. If anything, 'Compacta' is showier than its larger cousin because its color is more concentrated and dense.

It is interesting to note that while we grow firebush for its ornamental qualities, it has been grown for hundreds of years as a medicinal herb. Infusions from the leaves and stems have been used to relieve pain, reduce inflammation, heal wounds, reduce spasms, kill parasites and fungi, increase urination, reduce fever, and enhance immunity.

Hibiscus moscheutos
Swamp Mallow

Say: hi-BIS-kus mos-KEW-tos
Salt tolerance: Moderate
Size: 3–8 ft. tall/3–7 ft. wide
Origin: Eastern United States
Hardiness: USDA Zones 5–10

Family: Malvaceae (Mallow)
Other names: Hardy hibiscus, swamp hibiscus, swamp rose mallow
Propagation: Seeds; root division

'Luna Pink Swirl'

'Luna Red'

beneficial insects.

Many cultivars and hybrids are available. Look for cultivars or series such as 'Moy Grande', 'Lord Baltimore', 'Luna', 'Disco Belle', 'Southern Belle', and many more.

Most of the hardy swamp mallows available at nurseries are hybrids. Within the group is considerable variation in size, shape, and texture of the foliage, as well as the height of the plants. The main attraction is the fantastically huge dinner plate–sized flowers that range in color from white to pink to red. Some plants can grow to eight feet tall, but cultivars are available that grow only three to four feet tall. Although individual flowers last only one or two days, hundreds are produced, so the plant is almost constantly in flower.

Some tall plants may need support. Regular deadheading will maintain the attractiveness of the planting. Blossoms are loaded with nectar and pollen. Hummingbirds are frequent visitors, and certain native bees collect the pollen. The tall stems provide overwintering sites for

Culture Swamp mallow needs rich soil, consistent moisture, and full sun. Fertilize regularly for best growth and flowering, and mulch to maintain soil moisture. Cut dead stalks back in spring just before new growth emerges. Provide good air circulation in humid areas to prevent diseases, but protect from strong winds to minimize the risk of wind burn. Pinch growing tips to promote bushiness, and prune as desired to control height. Monitor for insects and control them as necessary.

Hibiscus mutabilis
Confederate Rose

Say: hi-BIS-kus mew-TAB-ill-iss
Salt tolerance: Slight
Size: 10–20 ft. tall/10–15 ft. wide
Origin: Southern China
Hardiness: USDA Zones 7–9

Family: Malvaceae (Mallow)
Other names: Cotton rose, Dixie rosemallow
Propagation: Cuttings (very easy in water or damp soil); seeds

Confederate rose lights up late fall landscapes throughout the South. Because this Chinese native has adapted to the South so well and the flower resembles a rose, it is referred to as a Confederate rose. The Confederate rose is a multistemmed large shrub or small tree. Single or double flowers four to six inches in diameter open white and change to light pink and then darker pink as they age. All colors are present at the same time.

While the Confederate rose tends to be treelike in Zones 9 and 10, in Zones 7 and 8 it is likely to get killed to the ground by the first hard freeze. The following spring it will resprout with even more vigor than before. The selection 'Plena' has double flowers that turn pink to red the second day. 'Rubra' has single deep pink to carmine blooms.

Legend has it that the flower changes color during the day because it soaks up blood that was spilled on the ground during the Civil War. The later in the day it becomes, the more blood the flower is able to absorb, so that by the end of the day it is nearly red.

Confederate rose is, along with other members of the hibiscus family, on some lists of edible plants. One source indicated that the root is edible but "very fibrousy and mucilaginous without very much flavor." It seems that if one were starving and nothing else was available to eat, Confederate rose might be considered. The leaves contain rutin, which has anti-inflammatory and other medicinal properties.

Culture Once Confederate rose is established in the landscape, it pretty much takes care of itself. Preference is for full sun or light, shifting shade. Although it appreciates moist, well-drained soil, it is quite drought tolerant. White flies, weevils, and caterpillars may be problematic.

Justicia brandegeana
Shrimp Plant

Say: jus-TEE-see-ah bran-dij-ee-AN-uh
Salt tolerance: Moderate
Size: 3–6 ft. tall/3–4 ft. wide
Origin: Mexico
Hardiness: USDA Zones 8–11

Family: Acanthaceae (Acanthus)
Other names: Shrimp bush, false hop
Propagation: Division of clumps;
   cuttings; seeds

bracts, including yellow, lime green or chartreuse, pink, and dark brick red. Selections with variegated leaves are available. Formerly the plant was named *Beloperone guttata.*

Justicia brandegeana attracts hummingbirds and is number four on Operation Rubythroat's list of exotic hummingbird plants.

Justicia is a genus of about 420 different species of plants. Other popular species include *Justicia betonica* (white shrimp plant) and *Justicia carnea* (Brazilian plume).

J. aurea (yellow jacobinia)

Shrimp plant grows in weakly branching clumps and blooms almost year-round in mild climates. The white flower, which has internal purple markings, projects from dark red to rusty brown bracts (modified leaves). The overlapping bracts form drooping, three- to seven-inch-long spikes that somewhat resemble large shrimp.

While shrimp plant is evergreen in mild climates, in the coldest part of its growing area, hard freezes kill it to the ground. It resprouts in spring, and plants can gradually increase to form large clumps. Cultivars include different colored flower

Culture For best growth, provide fertile, well-drained soil for shrimp plant. Although it is drought tolerant, it benefits from frequent watering, especially during hot weather. It does well in full to partial sun, but some protection from the hot afternoon sun keeps the bracts from fading. Containers can be overwintered in a protected place. Prune or pinch young plants to shape and promote bushiness, and cut back stems after bracts turn black or become unattractive. Shear the entire clump back to the ground to rejuvenate if growth becomes unattractive.

Turk's Cap

Say: mal-vuh-VIS-kus pend-yoo-lee-FLOR-us

Salt tolerance: Moderate

Size: 5–8 + ft. tall/5–8 ft. wide

Origin: Mexico, Central and South America

Hardiness: USDA Zones 8–11

Family: Malvaceae (Mallow)

Other names: Sleeping hibiscus, cardinal's hat

Propagation: Cuttings; layering

frost has killed them.

Wax mallow (*Malvaviscus arboreus* var. *drummondii*) is a closely related species that is native to Florida. Flowers are held more upright, and small, applelike fruits follow the flowers. This old-fashioned plant spreads by seeds and rhizomes and may be aggressive in favorable situations.

The nodding blooms of Turk's cap make it easy to understand why one of its common names is "sleeping hibiscus." The flowers hang from the bush like a hibiscus that might be sleeping, but it never awakens and unfurls its petals like the closely related tropical hibiscus. Two-inch-long, tubular flowers with projecting stamens and pistils may be red, pink, or white. Butterflies are attracted to the flowers and can be found hanging from the blossoms like an extended part of the flower.

This is another of the plants that get killed to the ground in winter in Zone 8. All spring and summer it grows, and in fall the blossoms appear. Hummingbirds are frequent visitors when the plants are in bloom. Remove dead stems after the

Culture Turk's cap blooms most prolifically in full sun but also tolerates shade. In shade it may become leggy and clamber over surrounding shrubs. It is easy to grow in just about any soil and is very drought resistant once established. Few pests bother this vigorous plant, and it is tolerant of environmental stresses. Tip-pruning the branches during the growing season will encourage branching and increased flowering.

Say: oh-don-toh-NEM-uh kus-pi-
DAY-tum
Salt tolerance: Slight to none
Size: 3–6 ft. tall/2–4 ft. wide
Origin: Central America
Hardiness: USDA Zones 8–11

Family: Acanthaceae (Acanthus)
Other names: Cardinal's guard,
scarlet flame
Propagation: Easy from tip cuttings
placed in moist soil

tendency to become invasive in areas where winter cold limits its growth.

This plant is sometimes listed as *Odontonema strictum.*

Firespike spends much of the summer growing to flowering size in Zone 8. Stiff, mostly unbranched stems shoot straight up, and large, avocado-like leaves lend a tropical feel to the garden. Six- to eight-inch-long leaves with wavy margins and long, pointed tips are characteristic. In fall, 12-inch spikes of bright red tubular flowers thrust up from the stems and attract the attention of butterflies and hummingbirds, as well as humans.

Firespike blooms in fall, when few other flowers are blooming in the garden. Planted in masses about two feet apart, it quickly fills in an area. Firespike has escaped cultivation in south Florida, but it shows no

Culture Firespike appreciates partial shade. Although it will grow well in full sun, the leaves tend to wilt and are lighter in color than shade-grown specimens. Moist, well-drained soil is preferred. Firespike is evergreen in the tropics but is killed to the ground by freezing weather. When it resprouts in spring, apply a bit of slow-release fertilizer to maintain the deep green color of the leaves. Water during periods of drought. Few pests and diseases are of concern. Prune to the ground in winter after frost has blackened the stems and foliage.

Plumbago auriculata
Plumbago

Say: plum-BAY-go aw-rik-yoo-LAY-tuh
Salt tolerance: Slight
Size: 6–10 ft. tall/8–10 ft. wide
Origin: South Africa
Hardiness: USDA Zones 8–11

Family: Plumbaginaceae (Leadwort)
Other names: Leadwort, skyflower
Propagation: Seeds; cuttings;
    division; layering

(*P. auriculata* var. *alba*) is available, and the cultivar 'Royal Cape' has intense cobalt blue flowers. Blue plumbago should not be confused with dwarf plumbago (*Ceratostigma plumbaginioides*), which is a groundcover plant that is hardy in Zones 5–9.

For subtropical areas, plumbago is a favorite shrub that blooms most of the year. Clusters of phloxlike flowers bloom in shades of blue. Flowers are tubular, but at the end of each tube, five petals flare out and flatten to display a one-inch blossom. If left to its own devices, the shrub becomes sprawling and vinelike. However, judicious pruning can make it more mounding and shrubby.

In Zone 8 plumbago often gets killed to the ground in winter, but it returns reliably in spring. Outside the limits of its hardiness range, it can be grown as a container plant and moved to a protected place during the winter. It is attractive in planters, where it cascades over the sides and provides a spot of color for sunny decks and patios.

Plumbago is frequented by butterflies, and it is one of the larval food plants for the Cassius blue butterfly. A white-flowered variety

Culture Plant plumbago in light, sandy, slightly acid soil with good drainage. Flowering is best in full sun. Prune regularly to keep it neat and within bounds if it is being grown as a shrub. Flowers are produced on new wood, so it can be pruned in late winter if the plant is unsightly. It is moderately drought tolerant, and few pests are of concern. An application or two of fertilizer during the growing season will encourage continuous growth and flowering.

Rotheca myricoides
Blue Butterfly Bush

Say: roh-THEE-kuh mir-ih-KOY-deez
Salt tolerance: Slight
Size: 3–10 ft. tall/3–6 ft. wide
Origin: East Africa (Kenya and Uganda)

Hardiness: USDA Zones 8–11
Family: Lamiaceae (Mint)
Other names: Blue butterfly clerodendrum, blue glorybower
Propagation: Easy from cuttings

Blue butterfly bush is an open shrub that is evergreen in frost-free climates. Four-inch-long, glossy leaves give the garden a tropical feel, and delicate blue flowers bloom from the tips of the branches in late summer to fall. Four petals of the flower are light blue, and the bottom petal, which is longer and somewhat cupped, is darker blue. Long, protruding purple stamens extend beyond the flower and arch outward and upward, suggesting to imaginative minds a butterfly in flight.

Rotheca myricoides was formerly placed in the *Clerodendrum* genus (and still is by some taxonomists). It is sometimes listed as *Clerodendrum ugandense* and may also be listed as *Rotheca myricoides* 'Ugandense'.

Culture Grow blue butterfly bush under the shifting shade of tall trees or on the eastern side of a building so that it gets morning sun. The plant will be killed to the ground at the first hard frost, but it is root hardy throughout Zone 8. Expect it to sprout in spring, and prune growing tips as stems emerge to encourage branching. Unpruned shrubs may grow long, gangly stems up to ten feet high. A frequently pruned shrub grows lower and denser, and has many more flowers. An option for those who live outside tropical areas is to grow blue glorybower in a container and move it to a protected place during the winter.

Senna pendula

Cassia

Say: SEN-nuh PEN-du-luh
Salt tolerance: Moderate
Size: 8–12 ft. tall/8–12 ft. wide
Origin: South America
Hardiness: USDA Zones 9–11

Family: Fabaceae (Pea or bean family)
Other names: Christmas senna, golden shower, senna
Propagation: Seeds; cuttings

Senna is a tall shrub that is covered with bright yellow flowers at a time

of year when little else is blooming. Stems are somewhat zigzag. The compound leaves have three to six pairs of leaflets, which are oblong with rounded tips. Flowers are bright yellow, about one or two inches across, and are borne in clusters near the stem tips. Yellow anthers (pollen sacs) are prominently held at the tip of long, curved filaments.

Although senna is evergreen in tropical regions, it gets killed to the ground by frost in much of the South. In spring prune to remove dead wood, or cut the stems off near ground level. Pinch the young shoots during the growing season to encourage branching and a greater number of flowers.

Senna pendula and *Senna bicapsularis* are different species, and both can be found growing in the South. However, the name *Senna bicapsularis* (syn. *Cassia bicapsularis*) is often misapplied, so it is likely that plants labeled with this name are really *Senna pendula.*

About 250–260 species of *Senna* exist. One may encounter coffee weed (*Senna occidentalis*), which invades fields and is a stubborn weed to eradicate. Another is the popular candlestick cassia (*Senna alata*), which can grow as tall as 15 feet in height and width. Golden spikes of blooms resembling candelabras are spectacular in the late fall landscape.

Senna is the larval plant of the sulphur butterflies, so it is a popular choice for butterfly gardens. It is listed by the Florida Exotic Pest Plant Council as a Category I exotic invasive species for central and south Florida. Remember, though, that some plants are invasive in one area but not in another. Senna is not listed as invasive in north Florida.

Culture Senna flowers best in full sun but will also perform reasonably well in partial shade. It is moderately drought tolerant and prefers well-drained but moist soil.

* See page 16.

Say: tek-OH-muh stanz
Salt tolerance: Slight
Size: 10–25 ft. tall/10–20 ft. wide
Origin: Central and South America, Mexico, southwestern United States

Hardiness: USDA Zones 8B–11
Family: Bignoniaceae (Bignonia)
Other names: Esperanza, yellow trumpet bush, yellow elder
Propagation: Seeds; cuttings

Attractive and fragrant golden yellow, trumpet-shaped flowers bloom in clusters at branch tips and forks, bending twigs and giving an arching effect. The flowers are about two inches long and one inch across with as many as 50 to a cluster. Compound leaves are glossy green and have serrated margins. In the Deep South where it is hardy, it begins blooming in July and continues in flushes throughout the growing season. Blooms are followed by four- to eight-inch stringbeanlike seedpods that hang in vertical clusters.

Yellow elder is evergreen in the tropics. Elsewhere it is killed to the ground in the winter, but the roots survive into the low 20s. Consequently, it never reaches the stature of the plants grown in the tropics but grows into a manageable shrub. Pruning the branch tips when growth begins in spring improves the shape by encouraging branching.

Tecoma stans var. *angustata* is more hardy and can be grown into Zone 7. The cultivar 'Gold Star' blooms much earlier than the species and grows between three and four feet tall. In 1999 'Gold Star' became one of the Texas Superstar plants. It earned a top rating for being a stunning, heat-tolerant Texas native bearing striking masses of golden yellow, trumpet-shaped flowers and dark green, glossy, divided leaves.

Culture Almost any soil will suit yellow bells. Full sun and well-drained soil are preferred. Plants are very drought tolerant.

Tibouchina urvilleana

Tibouchina

Say: tib-oo-KYE-nuh er-vill-ee-AY-nuh
Salt tolerance: None
Size: 10–15 ft. tall/10–15 ft. wide
Origin: Brazil
Hardiness: USDA Zones 8–11

Family: Melastomataceae
  (Melastoma)
Other name: Princess flower
Propagation: Cuttings

Dark green, lance-shaped, velvety leaves of tibouchina are distinctive. Prominent veins begin at the base of the leaf and extend to the tip, spreading out as they approach the center of the leaf and narrowing back down at the tip. Royal purple blossoms about three inches in diameter with prominent curly stamens are held above the foliage. Flowers open in succession from a cluster of red buds at the ends of each stem. Each cluster produces flowers for about two weeks. A flush of bloom is followed by a growth flush so that the plant continues to grow and bloom all season.

Tibouchina is a sprawling, evergreen shrub or small tree in areas where it does not get killed to the ground. In Zone 8 it is root hardy and returns each spring. In tropical areas it blooms year-round, but in Zone 8 it blooms in late summer and fall.

Several species of tibouchina exist and may become more available in the future. *Tibouchina granulosa,* commonly called the purple glory tree, is a popular container plant everywhere if it can be protected from frost. It is even less tolerant of cold than princess flower, and it grows larger and has bigger leaves and flowers. Tibouchina is invasive in Hawaii and the Far East.

Culture Tibouchina grows best in full sun and well-drained, acid soil. An occasional application of fertilizer will keep the shrub blooming vigorously. Rich, moist soil is preferred, but some drought is tolerated. Organic mulch is beneficial and will protect the roots during freezing weather. Pinch growth tips to encourage branching.

Chapter 4
Other Trees and Shrubs

These trees and shrubs have been added to the back of the book in the interest of space. They are no less important than other trees and shrubs listed in the book, but they are perhaps less common or less frequently chosen than some of the others. Nevertheless, these plants can fill a number of landscape needs.

Trees

Asimina triloba
Pawpaw

Say: uh-SIM-min-nuh try-LO-buh
Salt tolerance: Slight
Size: 10–15 ft. tall/10–15 ft. wide
Origin: Eastern United States
Hardiness: USDA Zones 5–9
Family: Annonaceae (Annona)
Other names: Indian banana, Hoosier banana
Propagation: Seeds (stratified in moist medium for 60 days at 41°F)

USDA-NRCS Plants Database

Flowers/fruits/foliage: Purplish-brown, broad, bell-shaped flower appearing before the leaves; fruit resembles a short, fat banana that is three to six inches long and hangs in clusters with two to nine fruits per cluster, first green but turning yellow and then brown as they ripen; deciduous foliage; alternate leaves five to eleven inches long and two to three inches wide; odor of green pepper when crushed.

Culture: Rich, well-drained soil; filtered sun or shade when young, tolerating more sun as it matures.

Comments: Largest edible fruit of any North American plant; roots depend on a symbiotic relationship with soil bacteria.

Calia secundiflora
Texas Mountain Laurel

Say: KAL-ee-uh sek-und-ee-FLOR-uh
Salt tolerance: Slight to none
Size: 15–20 ft. tall/10–12 ft. wide
Origin: Southeastern New Mexico to central and western Texas and Mexico
Hardiness: USDA Zones 7B–10A
Family: Fabaceae (Bean)
Other name: Mescalbean
Propagation: Seeds; cutting; layering; grafting

Flowers/fruits/foliage: Spring-blooming; clusters (racemes) of purple to blue wisteria-like flowers two to five inches long; fragrance of grape bubblegum; hairy seedpods up to eight inches long follow the flowers; open to reveal bright red seeds; thick, glossy, pinnately compound leaves

containing 5 to 13 leaflets each.

Culture: Full sun and well-drained soil; best adapted to the limestone soil of south and central Texas; very drought tolerant.

Comments: Evergreen shrub or small tree with a narrow, upright silhouette; deep root system; transplanting difficult; plant seeds where a tree is wanted.

Cladrastis kentukea
Yellowwood

Say: kluh-DRAS-tis ken-TUK-ee-uh
Salt tolerance: Unknown
Size: 30–50 ft. tall/40–50 ft. wide
Origin: Southeastern North America
Hardiness: USDA Zones 4–8
Family: Fabaceae (Pea)
Other name: Kentucky yellowwood
Propagation: Scarified seeds; cultivars budded to a seedling rootstock

Flowers/fruits/foliage: White, pendulous, terminal clusters of pealike flowers in late spring; cultivar 'Rosea' has pink flowers; fruit is a flattened seedpod two to four inches long; deciduous eight- to 12-inch compound leaves with seven to nine leaflets; yellow fall color.

Culture: Well-drained soil; full sun; tolerates alkaline soil.

Comments: Native on limestone cliffs and ridges but tolerant of acid soil; flowers in cycles of every two to five years; weak crotches may cause breakage as tree ages.

USDA-NRCS Plants Database

131

Cotinus obovatus
American Smoketree

Say: ko-TYE-nus ob-oh-VAY-tus
Salt tolerance: None
Size: 20–30 ft. tall/15–25 ft. wide
Origin: Southern United States
Hardiness: USDA Zones 5–8
Family: Anacardiaceae (Cashew)
Other name: Chittamwood
Propagation: Seeds (after stratification);
    cuttings; layering

USDA-NRCS Plants Database

Flowers/fruits/foliage: Seven- to 12-inch fuzzy clusters of insignificant, yellowish-green flowers in spring; billowy hairs attached to elongated stalks on the spent flower clusters turn smoky pink to purplish-pink, giving a smoky appearance; leaves five to six inches long and pinkish-bronze in youth mature to a dark blue-green; spectacular fall colors with shades of yellow, red, orange, or purple.

Culture: Full sun to partial shade; adaptable to adverse conditions; tolerant of wet soil, sand, drought, and compacted soil; occurs naturally in alkaline soil but can adapt to acid soil; flowers on three-year-old wood; dioecious, so male and female plants must be grown if seeds are to be produced; verticillium wilt troublesome.

Comments: Yellow to orange dye can be extracted from the inner bark; crushed foliage and twigs scented like Pine-Sol disinfectant; weak wood susceptible to storm damage.

Prunus cerasifera
Purple Leaf Plum

Say : PROO-nus sair-uh-SIFF-er-uh
Salt tolerance: Moderate
Size: 15–30 ft. tall/15–25 ft. wide
Origin: Western Asia, Caucasia
Hardiness: USDA Zones 4–9
Family: Rosaceae (Rose)
Other names: None
Propagation: Seeds; cuttings

Flowers/fruits/foliage: Fragrant pink to white flowers before the leaves in spring; edible, one-inch-diameter fruits produced on many cultivars; dark purple leaves that retain their vivid color throughout the summer on some cultivars.

Culture: Full sun in well-drained, acid soil; tolerant of slightly alkaline soil; moderately heat and drought tolerant; avoid mechanical damage and grow as vigorously as possible; remove suckers.

Comments: Fruit attracts birds and small mammals; many cultivars; suggested for the South is 'St. Luke', a cultivar found in Plant City, Florida, with a very low chill requirement.

Ptelea trifoliata
Common Hop Tree

Say: TEL-ee-uh try-foh-lee-AY-tuh
Salt tolerance: None
Size: 5–15 ft. tall/10–15 ft. wide
Origin: United States (widely distributed)
Hardiness: USDA Zones 4–9A
Family: Rutaceae (Rue or Citrus)
Other name: Wafer-ash
Propagation: Seeds, budding, layering, grafting

Flowers/fruits/foliage: Flowers inconspicuous and greenish-white, borne in terminal clusters appearing in early summer; fragrant, orange blossom–like fragrance; fruits are one-inch-diameter compressed tan "wafers," which are persistent unless consumed by wildlife; trifoliate leaves, four to six inches long, glossy and dark green on top but pale and hairy below; turn yellow in fall.

Culture: Partial shade to full sun in slightly alkaline to acid, well-drained but moist soil.

Comments: Fruit once used as a substitute for hops in beer-making; no pests or diseases of major concern; cultivars 'Aurea', with new leaves bright yellow fading to pale green, and 'Glauca', with blue-green foliage.

Rhus copallinum
Shining Sumac

Say: roos kop-al-EE-num
Salt tolerance: Moderate
Size: 3–25 ft. tall/5–15 ft. wide
Origin: Eastern half of the United States
Hardiness: USDA Zones 5–10
Family: Anacardiaceae (Cashew)
Other names: Winged sumac, flame leaf
Propagation: Division of suckers; seeds

Flowers/fruits/foliage: Clusters of greenish-yellow flowers borne in showy six- to ten-inch terminal clusters; berries attractive to many species of birds; dark green compound leaves 8 to 12 inches long and having 9 to 21 leaflets; brilliant orange-red fall color.

Culture: Tolerates dry, infertile soil; full sun to partial shade.

Comments: A frequent colonizer of disturbed sites; tolerant of urban areas and pollution; other species include Chinese sumac (*Rhus chinensis*), a loose-growing, flat-topped tree that bears yellowish-white flower clusters in summer and has colorful fall foliage and fruit; and smooth sumac (*Rhus glabra*), native to eastern North America.

133

Shrubs

Baccharis halimifolia
Salt Bush

Say: BAK-uh-riss hal-im-ih-FOH-lee-uh
Salt tolerance: High
Size: 5–12 ft. tall/5–7 ft. wide
Origin: Coastal areas of eastern United States
Hardiness: USDA Zones 5–9
Family: Asteraceae (Aster)
Other names: Groundseltree, salt marsh elder, sea myrtle
Propagation: Seeds; cuttings taken in summer

Flowers/fruits/foliage: Male and female flowers in terminal, branched clusters; appear as feathery white tufts about one-fourth to one-half inch long; fruits are dandelion-like, feathery, white bristles that give the plant a silvery look in early fall on female plants; alternate, bright green to gray-green simple leaves one to three inches long and coarsely toothed; nonshowy fall color; deciduous.

Culture: Sun to partial shade; tolerates range of soil types, including poor fertility and wet sites.

Comments: Multistemmed, irregular, open, airy shrub; can become leggy; best used as filler at edge of natural areas; very useful as a salt-tolerant hedge or screen; useful for reclaiming wet sites such as retention basins and drainage ditches; attractive to butterflies.

Ceanothus americanus
New Jersey Tea

Say: see-an-OH-thus a-mer-ih-KAY-nus
Salt tolerance: Unknown
Size: 3–4 ft. tall/3–5 ft. wide
Origin: Southern Canada, eastern, central, and southeastern United States
Hardiness: USDA Zones 4–8
Family: Rhamnaceae (Buckthorn)
Other names: Redroot, wild snowball, mountain sweet
Propagation: Seeds (after stratification); softwood cuttings

Flowers/fruits/foliage: Round clusters of tiny, fragrant, white flowers

appearing on long stalks at the stem tips or upper leaf axils in late spring; clusters of black fruit that form in late summer; leaves toothed, medium to dark green but gray and hairy below; each leaf about four inches long and distinctively ribbed with three prominent veins; young twigs noticeably yellow and stand out in winter.

Culture: Full sun to partial shade; average, dry to medium, well-drained soil; tolerates dry conditions and rocky soil.

Comments: Dried leaves have been used as a tea substitute; roots fix nitrogen; attracts hummingbirds, butterflies, and birds; useful in shrub borders or native plant gardens.

Conradina canescens
False Rosemary

Say: kon-ruh-DEE-na kan-ESS-kens
Salt tolerance: High
Size: 1–2 ft. tall/1–2 ft. wide
Origin: West Florida and adjacent Alabama
Hardiness: USDA Zones 7–10
Family: Lamiaceae (Mint)
Other names: Gray-leaved conradina, wild rosemary
Propagation: Seeds; softwood cuttings during the growing season

Flowers/fruits/foliage: Clusters of white to lavender, two-lipped flowers resembling small, pale lavender snapdragons bloom in spring; narrow, needlelike, aromatic leaves less than one inch long; olive green with grayish undersides.

Culture: Full sun, perfectly drained sandy soil.

Comments: Very drought and salt tolerant; contributes to the habitat of the beach mouse; flowers provide nectar for butterflies, hummingbirds, and bees; other species include *C. etonia* (Etonia rosemary), *C. glabra* (Apalachicola rosemary), *C. verticillata* (Cumberland rosemary), *C. grandiflora* (large-flowered rosemary), and *C. brevifolia* (short-leafed rosemary).

Exochorda racemosa
Common Pearlbush

Say: ek-so-KOR-duh ray-see-MO-suh
Salt tolerance: None
Size: 10–15 ft. tall/10–15 ft. wide
Origin: China
Hardiness: USDA Zones 4–8
Family: Rosaceae (Rose)
Other name: Pearlbush
Propagation: Cuttings; seeds

Flowers/fruits/foliage: Six to ten flowers about one and one-half inches wide are borne on three- to five-inch clusters (racemes) in early spring on previous season's growth; flowers white, five-petaled, cup-shaped, and nonfragrant; expanding buds resemble pearls; fruit a five-segmented brown capsule about one-third of an inch wide, which persists on the plant; alternate, simple, medium green leaves one to three inches long, which are serrated above the middle; deciduous but early to leaf out.

Culture: Sun to partial shade; prefers well-drained, loamy, acid soil.

Comments: Heat and drought tolerant; may become floppy and appear unkempt with age, but can be pruned severely to rejuvenate; cultivars include the hybrid forms 'The Bride' and 'The Pearl'.

Fothergilla gardenii
Dwarf Witch-Alder

Say: foth-er-GIL-la gar-DEN-ee-eye
Salt tolerance: Unknown
Size: 3–6 ft. tall/3–6 ft. wide
Origin: Southeastern United States
Hardiness: USDA Zones 4–8
Family: Hamamelidaceae (Witch-hazel)
Other names: Witch-alder, dwarf
    fothergilla
Propagation: Seeds; softwood tip
    cuttings; layering

Flowers/fruits/foliage: White, sometimes pink-tinged, bottlebrush-like spikes composed of stamens (flowers have no petals); one to two inches long; lightly fragrant; alternate, simple leaves, serrated margin toward the tip; brilliant fall color.

Culture: Moist, acid soil, rich in humus; partial shade.

Comments: *Fothergilla major* (large witch alder) is a larger-growing species; cultivars include 'Blue Mist', 'Mt. Airy', and 'Jane Platt'.

Heptacodium miconioides
Seven-Son Flower

Say: hep-tuh-KOH-dee-um mik-on-ee-OY-
    deez
Salt tolerance: Moderate
Size: 15–20 ft. tall/8–10 ft. wide
Origin: China
Hardiness: USDA Zones 5–9
Family: Caprifoliaceae (Honeysuckle)
Other names: None
Propagation: Seeds; softwood cuttings in
    spring

Flowers/fruits/foliage: Terminal clusters of fragrant, creamy white flowers in clusters of seven; flowers followed by showy display of small, purplish-red fruits with bright purple red calyxes (the usually green but sometimes showy part of a flower that lies underneath the petals and protects the buds); leaves narrow, shiny, ovate-oblong, and medium green, turning purple-bronze in fall.

Culture: Needs full sun for best flowering; tolerates a wide range of soils from dry and sandy to wet clays.

Comments: Fountain-shaped, multistemmed, deciduous shrub that can be trained to a single-trunked small tree; tan bark exfoliates to reveal attractive brown inner bark, providing good winter interest; use in shrub border or woodland garden; attracts bees and butterflies; sometimes called the "crape myrtle of the North."

Jasminum nudiflorum
Winter Jasmine

Say: JAZ-mih-num noo-dee-FLOR-um
Salt tolerance: Unknown
Size: 6–10 ft. tall/6–10 ft. wide
Origin: China
Hardiness: USDA Zones 6–10
Family: Oleaceae (Olive)
Other name: Hardy jasmine
Propagation: Cuttings during the growing
    season, layering (which occurs
    naturally where stems touch the
    ground)

Flowers/fruits/foliage: Nonfragrant, bright yellow, salver-shaped, one-inch flowers start blooming at the base of leafless stems in early winter and progress upward to the stem tips by late winter or early spring; bright green, glossy compound leaves divided into three oblong leaflets; deciduous.

Culture: Full sun for best flowers but also tolerates shade; tolerant of poor soil, moderately drought tolerant.

Comments: Fast-growing and can cover large areas over time when branches root where they touch the ground; use on slopes or above retaining walls, where trailing branches can cascade; cut back severely every three or four years to maintain shrub form; can be trained to climb 12 to 15 feet high on a support; cultivar 'Aureum' has leaves blotched with yellow.

Among the other species used in landscapes of the South are: *Jasminum multiflorum* (downy jasmine, Zones 9–11), a popular landscape shrub that has escaped cultivation in peninsular Florida; *J. mesnyi* (primrose jasmine, Zones 8–9), which is similar to *J. nudiflora* but larger in all its parts; *J. floridum* (showy jasmine, Zones 8–10), which extends the flowering season into the spring and is valued for its attractive foliage; and *J. officinale* (common white jasmine, Zones 8–10), with deliciously scented white flowers.

Caution*
Ligustrum japonicum
Ligustrum

Say: lig-GUS-trum juh-PON-ih-kum
Salt tolerance: Moderate
Size: Size: 8–12 ft. tall/15–25 ft. wide
Origin: Japan, eastern Asia
Hardiness: USDA Zones 8–10
Family: Oleaceae (Olive)
Other names: Japanese privet, wax-leaf
    privet
Propagation: Seeds; cuttings; named
    selections grafted onto seedling
    rootstock

Flowers/fruits/foliage: Terminal clusters of white flowers in spring with odor that some people find objectionable, as well as large quantities of pollen that wreak havoc with allergy sufferers; persistent fruits begin green and ripen to dull black; foliage glossy, evergreen, somewhat pear-shaped, and sharp-pointed at the tip.

Culture: Full sun to partial shade; wet to dry, well-drained soil; prune to maintain desired shape and size; treat for sooty mold and whitefly if necessary; reseeds readily; remove flowers and fruit to limit spread.

Comments: Often limbed up and grown as a small tree; many cultivars selected for varied ornamental characteristics; plants grafted onto *L. quihoui* preferred when available as protection against nematodes, which can be troublesome on sandy soil.

Has escaped cultivation and is invasive in many Southern states; *Ligustrum lucidum* very similar and also invasive; most invasive of all are *L. sinense* (including the variegated form) and *L. vulgare,* which should be avoided.

* see pg. 16

Skimmia japonica
Japanese Skimmia

Say : SKIM-ee-uh juh-PON-ih-kuh
Salt tolerance: Unknown
Size: 2–5 ft. tall/3–6 ft. wide
Origin: Japan, China, southeast Asia
  Hardiness: USDA Zones 7–9
Family: Rutaceae (Rue or Citrus)
Other name: Skimmia
Propagation: Seeds after pulp is removed; root cuttings in late summer and fall

Flowers/fruits/foliage: Red buds open to fragrant white flowers held in dense clusters (panicles); flowers followed by red berries; oblong leaves dark green above and yellow-green below; aromatic when bruised.

Culture: Partial shade to shade, may get bleached out in sun; prefers moist, acid, highly organic soil, but may also thrive in limestone soil.

Comments: Slow-growing evergreen shrub; one male plant per six female plants needed for good fruit set; male bears larger, more fragrant white flowers, but the female bears attractive berries; *Skimmia reevesiana* (Reeves skimmia) is similar, but lower growing, self-fertile, with dull crimson fruit; poisonous, causes cardiac arrest.

Image Credits

All images not credited are by the author.

Photographs

Aesculus pavia
John D. Byrd, Mississippi State University,
    Bugwood.org

Amelanchier arborea
Bill Cook, Michigan State University,
    Bugwood.org

Cornus kousa
Todd Boland, Research Horticulturist,
    University of Newfoundland
    Botanical Garden, Canada
The Dow Gardens Archive, Dow Gardens,
    Bugwood.org

Cotinus coggygria
The Dow Gardens Archive, Dow Gardens,
    Bugwood.org
www.provenwinners.com

Franklinia alatamaha
Janet Carson, University of Arkansas

Halesia diptera
Steve Hurst @ USDA-NRCS PLANTS
    Database
Chris Evans, River to River CWMA,
    Bugwood.org

Hamamelis virginiana
Chris Evans, River to River CWMA,
    Bugwood.org

Hovenia dulcis
Audrey Swindal, Florida Federation of
    Garden Clubs
J.S. Peterson @ USDA-NRCS PLANTS
    Database

Koelreuteria paniculata
J. S. Peterson @ USDA-NRCS PLANTS
    Database
Jim Hawk, Odessa, FL

Malus angustifolia
Kristina Simms, Bugwood.org
School of Renewable Natural Resources,
    LSU AgCenter
    2008–Jim L. Chambers

Parkinsonia aculeata
http://en.wikipedia.org/wiki/Parkinsonia_
    aculeata (Public Domain)

Pinckneya bracteata
Gil Nelson, PhD, Writer, Naturalist, and
    Educator
Jeff McMillian

Prunus angustifolia
Chris Evans, River to River CWMA,
    Bugwood.org

Stewartia malacodendron
Edmund R. Taylor, www.
    swallowtailgardendesigns.com
James Henderson, Gulf South Research
    Corporation, Bugwood.org

Buddleja alternifolia
Phillip Oliver

Clethra alnifolia
Ted Bodner Southern Science Society,
    Bugwood.org
www.parkseed.com 'Rosea'

Deutzia gracilis
Richard Webb, Garden Restoration,
    Bugwood.org
Chardonnay Pearls® www.provenwinners.
    com

Hibiscus syriacus 'Blue Bird'
www.waysidegardens.com

Hydrangea paniculata
www.waysidegardens.com 'Pinky Winky'
www.provenwinners.com 'Limelight'

Itea virginica
Chris Evans, River to River CWMA,
    Bugwood.org
www.provenwinners.com 'Little Henry'

Kalmia latifolia
Dow Gardens Archives, Dow Gardens,
    Bugwood.org

Kerria japonica
Phillip Oliver

Kolkwitzia amabilis
Rob Broekhuis (www.robsplants.com)
Phillip Oliver

Leucothoe axillaris
Richard Carter, Valdosta State University,
    Bugwood.org
Ted Bodner, Southern Weed Science
    Society, Bugwood.org

Lindera benzoin
The Dow Gardens Archive, Dow Gardens,
    Bugwood.org

Lyonia lucida
James H. Miller, USDA Forest Service,
    Bugwood.org
Richard Carter, Valdosta State University,
    Bugwood.org

Pieris japonica
The Dow Gardens Archive, Dow Gardens,
    Bugwood.org

Styrax americanus
Paul Redfearn @ MissouriState.edu
J.S. Peterson @ USDA-NRCS PLANTS
    Database

Weigela florida
 www.provenwinners.com 'Fine Wine'

Hibiscus moscheutos
www.provenwinners.com 'Luna Red'
    and 'Luna Pink Swirl'

Drawings

USDA-NRCS PLANTS Database / Britton,
N. L., and A. Brown. 1913. *An illustrated
flora of the northern United States,
Canada and the British Possessions.*

Asimina triloba (Pawpaw) Vol. 2:83
Baccharis halimifolia (Salt Bush) Vol.
    3: 445.
Ceanothus americanus (New Jersey
    Tea) Vol. 2:504.
Cladrastis kentukea (Yellowwood)
    Vol. 2: 343.
Cotinus obovatus (American
    Smoketree) Vol. 2: 485.
Fothergilla gardenia (Dwarf Witch-
    Alder) Vol. 2: 234.
Ptelea trifoliata (Common Hop Tree)
    Vol. 2: 445.
Rhus copallinum (Shiny Sumac) Vol.
    2: 481

Public Domain (wikimediacommons.org)
    Skimmia japonica (Japanese
    Skimmia)

Art by Joe Stoy
    Prunus cerasifera
    Calia secundiflora
    Conradina canescens
    Exochorda racemosa
    Heptacodium miconioides
    Jasminum nudiflorum
    Ligustrum japonicum

Map on page 17 courtesy of the
    USDA's Agricultural Research Service,
    USDA-ARS

Bibliography

Bender, Steve. *The Southern Living Garden Book.* Birmingham, AL: Oxmoor House, 1998.

Black, Robert J. and Edward F. Gilman. *Landscape Plants for the Gulf and South Atlantic Coasts, Selection, Establishment, and Maintenance.* Gainesville, FL: University Press of Florida, 2004.

Dirr, Michael A. *Hydrangeas for American Gardens.* Portland, OR: Timber Press, 2004.

Dirr, Michael A. *Manual of Woody Landscape Plants, Their Identification, Ornamental Characteristics, Culture, Propagation, and Uses.* Champaign, IL: Stipes Publishing, 1990.

Dirr, Michael A. *Viburnums: Flowering Shrubs for Every Season.* Portland, OR: Timber Press, 2007.

Halfacre, R. Gordon and Anne Rogers Shawcroft. *Landscape Plants of the Southeast.* Raleigh, NC: Sparks Press, Inc., 1989.

Jarrett, Amanda. *Ornamental Tropical Shrubs.* Sarasota, FL: Pineapple Press, Inc., 2003.

Kurz, Herman and Robert K. Godfrey. *Trees of Northern Florida.* Gainesville, FL: University Press of Florida, 1993.

Nelson, Gil. *Florida's Best Native Landscape Plants.* Gainesville, FL: University Press of Florida, 2003.

Nelson, Gil. *The Shrubs and Woody Vines of Florida: A Reference and Field Guide.* Sarasota, FL: Pineapple Press, Inc., 1996.

Odenwald, Neil and James Turner. *Identification Selection and Use of Southern Plants for Landscape Design.* Baton Rouge, LA: Claitor's Publishing Division, 1987.

Osorio, Rufino. *A Gardener's Guide to Florida's Native Plants.* Gainesville, FL: University Press of Florida, 2001.

Rushing, Felder. *Tough Plants for Florida Gardens.* Nashville, TN: Cool Springs Press, 2004.

Seidenberg, Charlotte. *The Wildlife Garden, Planning Backyard Habitats.* Jackson, MS: University Press of Mississippi, 1995.

Stebbins, Mark K. *Flowering Trees of Florida.* Sarasota, FL: Pineapple Press, Inc., 1999.

Toby, John D., Burks, Cantrell, Garland, et al. *Florida Wetland Plants: an Identification Manual.* Tallahassee, FL: Department of Environmental Protection. 1998.

Wasowski, Sally with Andy Wasowski. *Gardening with Native Plants of the South.* Dallas, TX: Taylor Publishing, 1994.

Watkins, John V. and Herbert S. Wolfe. *Your Florida Garden.* Gainesville, FL: University Press of Florida, 1978.

Websites and Publications from
Cooperative Extension Services at:

Auburn University and Alabama A&M
    University, www.aces.edu/
Clemson University, Clemson, South
    Carolina, www.clemson.edu/
    extension/
Louisiana State University, www.
    agctr.lsu.edu/
Mississippi State University, www.
    msucares.com/
North Carolina State University and
    NC A&T University, www.ces.
    ncsu.edu/
Oklahoma State University, http://
    pods.dasnr.okstate.edu/
Texas A&M University, http://
    texasextension.tamu.edu/
University of Arkansas. www.uaex.
    edu/
University of Florida, http://edis.ifas.
    ufl.edu/
University of Georgia, www.ces.uga.
    edu/

www.floridata.com: An online
    encyclopedia

USDA-NRCS. 2007. The Plants
    Database (http://plants.usda.
    gov). National Plant Data Center,
    Baton Rouge, LA 70874–4490
    USA.

Index

Page numbers in brackets indicate photographs that do not accompany that plant's main text entry.